A DATE WITH DEATH

ACKNOWLEDGEMENTS AND APOLOGIES

Tragedy has been defined as: 'The disaster which comes to those who represent and who symbolize, in a peculiarly intense form, those flaws and short-comings which are universal in a lesser form.'

It was indeed the *intensity* of Jane Andrews' flaws that was extraordinary – for her flaws themselves were rather typical. At first Jane suffered from little more than insecurity and unfulfilled longings. She slowly transformed herself into a person that demonstrated greed, vanity, self-obsession, and finally promiscuity, brutality, and deceit. None of these flaws are particularly unusual. What made them fatal in this tragic case was their degree of intensity.

By studying Jane Andrews' strange journey into corruption and possibly madness, perhaps we can identify universal lessons about relationships and even about ourselves. I understand that this book will cause some pain and I would like to begin by apologizing to those most affected by the case.

For Thomas Cressman the pain ended with his death, but for the Cressman family – that is when the suffering began. I want to apologize to Barbara and Harry Cressman for any additional pain that this book may cause, and to thank them for their kindness and support. I would especially like to express my admiration for the bravery and elegance that Barbara displayed throughout the process of fighting for justice for her son's memory, as well as her patience in helping me with the development of the manuscript.

I want to apologize to Jane's parents, as well. I was deeply impressed and moved by their selfless support of their daughter throughout the trial and I know that they are among the greatest victims of this tragedy. I am sure that this narrative will sadden them, and I am sorry for that.

I can imagine that the Duchess of York will shake her head sadly as she picks up this book and wonder 'Is Starkie going to blame me for this too?' I am not. And I want to apologize to those readers that bought this book hoping I would do so.

I would like to commend Scotland Yard for its extreme professionalism throughout this case, and particularly I would like to offer my sincere thanks and admiration to Detective Sergeant Rory Beeson and Detective Chief Inspector Jim Dickie for their kindness toward me during my time as a witness, and for their assistance in developing the manuscript.

Richard Kay has been known as the most honorable journalist in Britain. A handshake from Richard is considerably more valuable than a contract from those lesser men who envy him. I want to thank Richard Kay for his friendship and the *Daily Mail* for their integrity.

The entire team at Mainstream Publishing demonstrated great enthusiasm and enormous dedication throughout the process of developing this book. I would like to thank Bill Campbell for his enthusiasm, Deborah Kilpatrick for her outstanding editing, Tina Hudson for the first book jacket I have ever loved, and the entire team at Mainstream for their support.

I would like to thank my employer Anthony Riotto for his generosity in making his offices available to Scotland Yard and allowing me time for the trial. Also, I want to thank him for his guidance and friendship.

Finally I would like to thank those close friends that listened and commented so patiently on the various iterations of my manuscript: Cindy Koury, Patty Rios, Mark Mauriello, Alexis Swift, and most of all my mother, Tina Starkie.

A DATE WITH DEATH

The Fatal Transformation
of Jane Andrews,
Royal Confidante Turned Killer

ALLAN STARKIE

MAINSTREAM
PUBLISHING

EDINBURGH AND LONDON

To *all* the victims

First published in Great Britain in 2001 by
MAINSTREAM PUBLISHING COMPANY
(EDINBURGH) LTD
7 Albany Street
Edinburgh EH1 3UG

ISBN 1 84018 505 8

A catalogue record for this book is available
from the British Library

Typeset in Berkeley and Gill
Printed and bound in Great Britain by
Butler & Tanner Ltd, Frome and London

CONTENTS

CHAPTER ONE

METHOD OR MADNESS?

You said I killed you — haunt me, then! The murdered *do* haunt their murderers, I believe. I know ghosts *have* wandered on earth. Be with me always — take any form — drive me mad! Only do not leave me alone in this abyss, where I cannot find you! Oh God it is unutterable! I *cannot* live without my life! I *cannot* live without my soul.

IT HAD BEEN NINE YEARS since Jane Dunn-Butler and I recited those haunting lines from the vintage edition of *Wuthering Heights* she had given me as token of our relationship and our shared admiration for the tortured passions described in Emily Brontë's troubled work. Now, nine years later, she had turned those words into her own Victorian tragedy.

Thomas Cressman lay silently next to his bed. As was his custom, in preparing to go to bed he wore only his boxer shorts and had removed his contact lenses. Thomas was extremely short-sighted and waited until he was ready for sleep before removing his lenses. He lay face down with one leg and both arms pinned beneath him, and the other leg draped over the edge of his bed, looking as if he were about to force himself up from a deep sleep. Two pillows covered his head. In his right hand he clutched the long blade of the kitchen knife that had killed him. He had succeeded in withdrawing the blade from his chest before losing consciousness. His fingers bore numerous lesions from the sharp blade he had clawed from his breast. Above his left eye, on his upper forehead, was a small, vertical wound, so clean and straight that it appeared to have been inflicted by a knife. It was only after examination that it was concluded it had come from the powerful blow of a cricket bat. The sheets, walls and pillows were covered in blood, for the chest wound was deep. Entering through the right lung, the knife had plunged its full length of nine inches diagonally into the pulmonary sac of the heart.

Thomas lay quietly and quite alone in the darkened room with its drawn curtains and closed door, which had been tied shut from the outside with the cord of his lover's bathrobe – a precautionary measure. In fact, the only disturbance was the occasional ringing of the telephone, which increased in frequency as his mother began to grow concerned. Thomas and his girlfriend Jane had recently returned from his mother's villa in the South of France, and Thomas was an attentive son who returned her calls promptly. Finally, after two days of mounting anxiety, his mother was able to reach Thomas's employee and ask him to check on her son's absence.

Thomas's office was across the street from his Fulham town house. It was there that Tim Kent arrived early on Monday morning. Opening the door, he was surprised to find that the lights and computer were on, while the security alarm was turned off. Tim sensed that something was terribly wrong. 'It felt weird all day,' he recollected. 'I kept getting shivers down my spine. People kept phoning.' Finally, on the prompting of Mrs Cressman, Tim reluctantly crossed the street, unlocked the door of Thomas's home and climbed the stairs to the first-floor bedroom shared by Thomas and his girlfriend of two years. When he reached the top of the landing he was shocked to see that the bedroom door was tied shut from the outside. The bloodstained cord of a bathrobe had been used to secure the door handle to the stairway banister, as if there were something inside which needed to be kept prisoner. With shaking hands, Tim untied the ominous cord and entered the darkened chamber. He recalled: 'There were clothes all over the floor. Something caught my eye and I looked round to the right. There was blood all over the floor, the sheets and walls. I froze completely, then turned and ran downstairs.'

The sight that terrified Tim and caused him to flee was Thomas's bloodied face, peering from under the pillows that covered his head. Tim was unprepared for the ghastly sight that confronted him, but even the seasoned Scotland Yard detectives investigating the case froze upon seeing the bathrobe cord. These hardened professionals from the Belgravia Station had seen many examples of the darkness that lurked beneath the lavish façades of London's social élite. Yet they gazed at each other and simultaneously breathed one word: 'Demons'. The meaning of that cryptic word and the heinous context in which it might fit are essential in understanding what possibly occurred in the moments following Thomas's date with death.

Jane, Thomas's girlfriend, had disappeared. With a stunned public gazing on every movement of the chase, Scotland Yard mounted a national search for Jane, somehow reminiscent of the O.J. Simpson flight that riveted the American public. The operation was codenamed Operation Rhossili and included the circulation of Jane's photo to all British ports and airports.

During the chase the people closest to Jane were questioned. Her neighbours reported that she was last seen watering plants outside the house on Saturday morning, only a matter of hours before the violent scene would be enacted. What thoughts were going through her mind during that calm pastoral moment? Her parents had heard nothing from her. Her ex-husband, Christopher Dunn-Butler, claimed to be 'absolutely stunned' at her disappearance. Jane's former employer, mentor and friend, the Duchess of York, interrupted her visit to the Wedgwood factory in Staffordshire to say that she was 'deeply worried' about Jane's whereabouts and that the two had remained in contact and 'on good terms' since Jane's mysterious dismissal in October 1996 after nine years of service.

Despite these statements of surprise, Jane's mobile phone records indicate that she had contacted Christopher, the Duchess and several other friends after Thomas's death. It was actually Jane's strange decision to continue to communicate with her friends that resulted in her ultimate capture. Beginning on Monday evening, Jane began a series of calls and text messages to her friend Lucinda Sharp. They were disturbed and confused calls, in which Jane first feigned ignorance of Thomas's death and then threatened suicide. Lucinda called the police and for the ensuing days was coached through her strange conversations by detectives who sat by her side throughout.

Again, one is reminded of the pursuit of O.J. Simpson, especially the strange car ride in which he drove with a gun pointed at his own head while a concerned police force desperately tried to prevent him from pulling the trigger. In this case Lucinda recalls, 'Jane kept screaming that she was going to kill herself, and I could tell that she was serious.' At times 'Jane got hysterical, at one point she was going to drive off Beachy Head [the famous suicide place near Eastbourne].'

The police were using hi-tech tracking devices to detect the origin of Jane's telephone signals, but were still unable to locate her. Scotland Yard made a national appeal asking the public to help find Jane. Meanwhile, Lucinda tried to keep her on the telephone and recalls, 'I tried to get her to tell me where she was but she said she didn't know.' The drama reached a crescendo on Tuesday, when Jane announced that she was taking a bottle of tablets. Fortunately, Lucinda had been able to convince Jane to describe her location and was thus able to guide the police to Cornwall.

Thomas had been killed some time in the late evening of Saturday, 16 September. It took until 6.45 the following Wednesday morning before a sleeping Jane Andrews was found in her car in Cornwall. The car was parked at a lay-by on the A38 at Liskeard. So Jane, the poor girl from the north-east town of Grimsby, who had tried so hard to escape her roots, took her last ride towards the south-western tip of England, as though she were still trying to distance herself from her past. She drove from her Emily Brontë obsession to the land of the equally romantic Daphne du Maurier, whose life and stories also influenced her malleable mind.

She had kept her promise and had taken a large number of Nurofen tablets. Jane was taken to Derriford Hospital, Plymouth, where it was determined that the pills were non-lethal. She remained there for treatment and then, after her release from the hospital, was transported to Belgravia Station where, on 23 September, she was charged with murder.

Jane was remanded to Holloway Prison, a woman's prison in north London where she was incarcerated with thieves, prostitutes and drug dealers. Her designer clothes were replaced by a blue tracksuit that she covered in white overalls when she performed her £6-a-week job cleaning the prison hallways and bathrooms. It was far removed from her former, highly publicised royal life as dresser and confidante to the Duchess of York. When she protested, 'I only drink bottled water', the guards simply shrugged their shoulders. Imagine the contrast between the last nine years of her life and what she experienced during her months in jail.

On 12 December a benevolent court set her free on bail. The terms were a sum of £40,000 and a curfew between 8.00 p.m. and 8.00 a.m. Additionally, she had to report twice weekly to the police. Perhaps the cruellest condition was the court's insistence that she return to her parents' home in Grimsby – the very place she seemed to have tried the hardest to escape. So, social-climbing Jane was imprisoned in the home of her roots, the small apartment of her social worker mother and carpenter father, and the world was to be clearly reminded of her humble origins. When she emerged from prison she bore little resemblance to the fashionable Lady Jane of old. Wearing black trousers and a black hooded top she appeared gaunt and silent, carrying a copy of Terry Waite's autobiography of his time as a Beirut hostage, *Taken on Trust*.

In the ensuing investigation, after the obligatory false trails and dead-ends (which included her early claim that Thomas was being blackmailed), Jane confessed to having killed her lover; yet the nature of the killing evolved into two diametrically opposed versions. The prosecution and the defence were forced to face-off to determine whether Jane was a victim or a predator: whether Thomas had so abused her that she feared for her safety and felt that she needed the protection of a cricket bat and butcher knife to sleep safely; or, whether Jane had learned that Thomas would never marry her and, in a scorned rage, murdered him cold-bloodedly.

Jane claims that she was awakened by Thomas's violent attack and grabbed the bat, striking him in self-defence. This only stunned and angered him and so, reaching for the knife, she pleaded for him to draw back – he fell forward, impaling himself. Unsure whether he was alive, Jane ran out of the room and, terrified that he might be following, tied the door closed with the rope of her bathrobe.

The prosecution has another version of the events of that fatal night. They believe that during the prior two weeks in the South of France, Thomas had unequivocally decided that he would never marry Jane. After a dramatic Saturday filled with arguments and threats of suicide, Jane waited for Thomas to prepare for sleep. She watched him remove his lenses – making himself vulnerable – and as he began to doze off struck him on the forehead with the bat. It is difficult to knock a person unconscious with a frontal blow, and if this version is true, Thomas would have been aware of what was transpiring, though stunned and virtually powerless to defend himself, barely able to achieve a kneeling position on the centre of the bed before Jane plunged the knife into his chest.

According to the prosecution, Jane then left the room and tied the door shut from the outside. Now comes the explanation of the term 'Demons'. Contract killers are professionals and do not fear the corpse of their victims but first-time killers are terrified of the dead body and will often lock or bar the door. As part of a society weaned on horror movies, the novice killer is frightened of the demons of the deceased.

Even the seasoned detectives, however, could not then have been aware of the degree to which Jane had been influenced by the supernatural, how the years in the household of the Duchess had been filled with purported ghostly events, communications from the dead and the spectre of tangible supernatural forces playing events in our daily lives. In Sarah's speech at the memorial service for her stepfather, Hector Barrantes, she quoted the lines, 'Death is nothing at all. I have only slipped away into the next room.' Was this not literally the case now with Thomas? Was he not truly in 'the next room'? Through the years of fortune-tellers, astrologers and communications from the grave, Jane had developed a strong respect for the power of the supernatural. Yes, 'demons' would have scared her. Later the prosecution grew to believe that Jane had tied the cord to 'rig the crime scene', that, seeking an alibi or mitigating factor, she simply wished to create the perception that she had something to fear.

Regardless of the validity of the two theories, some things are very clear. Whether afraid of the vengeance of a living or dead Cressman, Jane found the time to wash herself, dress and even write two notes to her parents. The missives are as difficult to interpret as the crime. The nebulously worded notes seem to be begging for forgiveness – but for what? Was Jane asking her parents to forgive the murder or her planned suicide? During the crucial hours leading up to her arrest, Jane never contacted the authorities, but managed to spend hours on her telephone. What does this indicate? Most of these questions have been answered during the trial and you already know the verdict of the jury. But the truth may be more complex than the barristers were able to define, involving the metamorphosis of the personality of an impressionable, ambitious young woman, corrupted by power, insatiable passions and privileges.

When I received the call from Detective Sergeant Beeson asking me to tell him about my relationship with Jane Dunn-Butler (as she was known during her 'royal years'), I was drawn deep into the past, through the volumes of my fading diaries, back almost a decade to when I first met Jane. I would have to reassess those bittersweet memories of the years in which I was so close to her and her mistress and see if I could understand the change in her, and come to my own understanding of what she had become.

Americans hold Scotland Yard in awe and reverence. Hollywood has not been unkind to the Yard and so my expectations were high when the FBI and Interpol told me they had given permission for two senior inspectors to come to America and interview me. The famous Detective Chief Inspector Jim Dickie, with his colleague Detective Sergeant Beeson, would personally conduct the interview.

I remember my first telephone exchange with Detective Sergeant Beeson after I had delayed returning his persistent calls for many days. 'How should I address you, Detective Sergeant?' I asked. 'Call me Rory,' was his disarming answer. With charm and patience, he slowly coaxed me out of my reluctance to reopen the past and revisit those pivotal five years in the lives of Jane and the Duchess.

It is a little disconcerting to have Scotland Yard reach across the Atlantic to find a person, so I asked, 'How did you locate me?' Rory answered, 'The Cressman family called us and asked us to speak with you.' I felt sorry for the family. I had not met Tommy (as he apparently liked to be called) but had heard nice things about him. I knew that he was respected in his industry and loved by his family. It had also become apparent that his reputation was being tarnished posthumously by the allegation that he had beaten Jane. Although I had no way of knowing if this were the case, I could certainly understand that the family would be grateful for any information I could provide about Jane's character.

'What do you want from me?' I finally asked with resignation. After all, I had not spoken to Jane in several years, while the Duchess and I had ended our relationship on difficult terms, fighting a media battle as we simultaneously defended our two versions of the events we had chronicled in our respective books. Although Sarah avoided ever appearing on the same talk shows as me, we nevertheless took unnecessary stabs at one another and it was not until the recent death of her mother that we again exchanged letters. I had tried to put our years together safely in my past and I was not expecting to have Scotland Yard draw me back into them. By way of explanation, Rory said: 'We were told by the Cressman family that you knew Jane very well and that you had some strange experiences with her.' 'Yes,' I had to agree, 'I knew her well.'

I had first met Jane in the early autumn of 1992 during a trip in which she accompanied the Duchess to Germany. Sarah was researching a book on Queen Victoria and Jane was her companion. It was barely six weeks after the infamous South of France photos had been published, in which my business partner and best friend John Bryan managed to indelibly engrave his image on the world's collective consciousness by linking his tongue to the toe of the topless Duchess. Sarah was devastated by the public reaction and needed friends. Jane and I were to be by her side for a myriad of trips, events and confessions that would last for the next four years of my life. For me to say, then, 'I knew her well' was both an understatement and a half-truth; there was very little of Jane – or should I say of a true and consistent Jane – to know.

In 1992 Jane appeared to be an empty, shapeless vessel eager to accept the liquid that was poured into it. Clear and malleable, her personality and even her appearance seemed to take on the form, expression and beliefs of the stronger personality of the Duchess. I was not alone in my feelings about Jane. Even after many years of service, when asked about Jane, the Duchess replied, 'I don't really know who Jane is.'

In the early portion of this narrative it is astonishing how little Jane is involved in the action. It is only after the story progresses to the point in which Jane has begun to emulate her mistress's personality that she truly begins to emerge as a character. It is important, therefore, to illustrate the strong characteristics of Sarah's personality so that it will become clear later on to what extent Jane imitated them.

Sarah was a tormented soul in the fall of 1992 and in the ensuing years she went through frequent and traumatic personality vacillations as she tried to rediscover herself. Sarah was so intent on trying to win acceptance that she seemed to accommodate the expectations of whomever she was trying to please. When I pointed this behaviour out to her, we collectively named it the 'chameleon effect'. Ironically, in her own memoirs published five years later Sarah would paraphrase my nickname and dub herself 'the Chameleon Queen'. Through Sarah's many manifestations, Jane seemed to study, then reproduce the ever-changing moods, mannerisms and beliefs of her mistress. There is a wonderful film called *All About Eve* in which Eve, a seemingly mousy, and victimised vagrant, is sponsored, employed and mentored by a tempestuous ageing actress played by Bette Davis. While ostensibly kowtowing and worshipping her benefactress, she was in fact constantly studying, subtly undermining and coveting the fame, friends and possessions of her mistress. Eve had no real substance except as a copy of her idol. She ultimately succeeded in making a convincing copy of the original at a huge cost. Within several months of meeting Jane, I began to think of her as an 'Eve' figure and that comparison grew in poignancy as the years went by.

And so I can only partially say, 'I knew her well', for there was not a whole, pre-existing entity to really know. I knew the receptacle – and I watched it change its colour and form until it resembled nothing so much as a confused copy of a person who herself lacked a clear self-identity. In a sense Jane had become the caricature of confusion – the imperfect imitation of a chameleon.

'We heard that she had a relationship with you,' continued the detective. 'We heard that she might have stalked you,' he added tentatively. This was an even more difficult question to answer, so I kidded him to break the ice by replying, 'Not as much as you have Rory,' trying to make fun of his indefatigable, unceasing messages until I finally had answered his calls. 'She was sort of obsessed with me, Rory, but she was never violent, or . . .' I paused before saying the words 'pushy' or 'frightening', for in truth she could be both of those things. I had sensed danger from the very beginning of our relationship, but it was a strange, indescribable fear that there would be psychological damage and injury if I succumbed to her advances, rather than a feeling that I personally was at risk. I felt a volcano of potential explosiveness in Jane, but I assumed that she would direct the destruction upon herself.

And so I tried haltingly to explain this to Scotland Yard. I tried to tell Rory that Jane was not only obsessed with copying Sarah, or sleeping with me, but that she was highly influenced by the supernatural and passionate forces that seemed to so interest Sarah. I wanted to convey that if there were anything that was purely Jane, it was a sense of longing and unfulfilled – perhaps even undefined – desire. I felt sure that were she to fixate the goal of this desire on any one person, there could be trouble and disappointment. Ultimately, I abridged my comments to focus on certain unnerving events that had transpired and these events seemed to be of the utmost importance to the case for the prosecution. Consequently, permission was granted for Rory and Detective Chief Inspector Dickie to spend a week in New York, with the purpose of trying to learn the pattern of Jane's behaviour.

When Rory announced that they would be coming, my first response was to ask, 'Will you be bringing a psychologist?' I had almost added 'and a priest', for in truth it sometimes seemed that Jane was *possessed* by figures from the past, or at least by the persona of the Duchess of York. 'No, just my supervisor and myself,' answered a contrite Rory.

'But you don't understand,' I protested. 'This is not simply a case of taking a deposition about clear facts. It is an interpretation of a strange metamorphosis in the psyche of a human being. The very questions that are asked need to be asked by a qualified psychologist.'

'I understand,' responded the patient detective. 'I assure you that your statement will be read by the appropriate people, and that might well include a psychologist.'

I tried in vain to protest, but in the end agreed to assist them by answering the questions that seemed most pertinent to them. I was told then, and understood, that Jane was not pleading insanity and, indeed, I would not have categorised her as insane. What I meant then and still believe is that Thomas's death, regardless of the verdict, was in some way linked to the evolution of Jane's values and the metamorphosis of her personality; it was these fundamental changes in Jane that either encouraged her to remain with a dangerous man or prompted her to murder the lover who shattered the illusory world in which she lived. For I watched Jane follow her mistress into an imaginary world populated by improbable protagonists gorged with insatiable passions. Vulnerable, impressionable Jane was swept away, swept into a world of dead queens, still mourning their undying love, into the Yorkshire Moors and up to Penistone Crag, where a distraught Heathcliff resolutely awaited the ghost of his lost Catherine.

Jane was carried into a fairytale land in which the dead existed alongside the living, where anything seemed possible and where the divisions between life and death, and right and wrong became so hazy that four of us – *four of us* – from the Duchess's inner circle would be arrested. Three would spend time in prison. And Sarah, almost prophesying this strange fate that awaited us, would often say, ' I will always be there for you. If you get into trouble, I will be there to bail you out of prison.' I do not mean to imply that Sarah was in any way responsible for the arrests of her lover, her dresser, her business associate and myself. But there was some common denominator either in her selection of friends or in the razor's-edge existence that we shared, which undeniably resulted in such carnage.

I used the remaining time until Rory and Jim arrived to refresh my memory on the strange events that occurred during those fascinating years with Sarah and Jane. I still had my infamous diaries of those years, seven leather-bound volumes in which I would pour out my revelations as I experienced the fast-track world of the social élite. These diaries had prompted an angry British press to accuse me of having spied on Sarah for five years, when from the beginning she had never discouraged me from being the scribe of our relationship. I had Sarah's diaries from our trips as well as the many letters she had written to me over the years, and I was able to find some of Jane's pathetic missives and even some of the gifts she had given to me. So I was well prepared for the visit – or so I thought.

I had reasoned that the fact that two policemen were coming indicated the possibility of them acting as a 'good cop, bad cop' team. Yet I was uncertain why they would feel the need to treat me as if it were an interrogation and not the interview of a cooperative witness. My secretary announced their arrival in a frightened little voice. They were accompanied by a New York detective who was to act as liaison and also as a sign of respect for their rank. He was a small, dark-haired, typical New York detective with a thick Brooklyn accent and an animated manner. Rory stood next to him and greeted me with a smile. He was about my age and had kind, warm blue eyes. Standing to the side, tall and formal, was Detective Chief Inspector Dickie. He looked as if central casting had chosen an actor that represented the American stereotype of the British Inspector. Jim

Dickie is tall with thick, grey hair, well groomed and elegant. His piercing blue eyes immediately fix upon you and one gets the sensation that he is looking deep into your soul, as if he quickly sees through any subterfuge or excuse and is already inventorying your sins, like the Prince of Darkness about to harvest the fresh soul of another secret sinner. I supposed he would play the bad cop.

We sequestered ourselves in my conference room and the questioning began. For several days we would be together and the theme would always follow the same pattern. Jim would ask a terse question and expect a simple response. I would try to explain that the answers were complex and needed to be placed in a context. I would ultimately appeal to Rory, who would then explain the resolve of the formidable Dickie and politely request that I limit my answers to fact. And so with looks of impatience and many requests for abridgement, I took them through the early days with Jane and Sarah. I tried to explain the profound influence that *Wuthering Heights* and the diaries of Queen Victoria had on Jane. Jim wanted facts, so I told of her strange obsession with me, of her pathetic attempts at what could be classified as stalking. Finally, the NY detective summarised the situation in what provided the solitary example of comic relief. In those thick Italian-American tones that only exist in Brooklyn, he pronounced: 'So, let me re-capit-two-late. The woman dinks she is like some fuckin' Heat-cliff charac-ta, but she has it ra-voiced, and you are Caty, and so she lives in this crazy woy-ld, so when her boyfriend don't do the right ding she offs him like some Romeo and Juliet shit or somethin'.'

'Exactly!' I exploded, trying hard to keep a straight face. In actuality, he had it about right.

'I know my classics,' was his proud response. In fact, after the week ended he was so pleased with himself that he offered me his card with his beeper number on the back. 'You treated us good – hold on to this,' he offered.

The week resulted in the compression of a very complicated story into a four-page statement. As I signed it, I guess Jim could see that I was not convinced that it adequately summarised my points, but it was pure fact and that was what they wanted. 'Allan, no one can write down your story on a statement,' he said consolingly. 'Only you can say it and you will get your chance, but we can't write it – we want just the pure facts. Your story needs to be written as a book.'

He was right.

CHAPTER TWO

THE SEDUCTION

'[Allan] greeted two frightened, rather timid (can you believe?) women . . .
my trusted Jane Dunn-Butler, who kindly agreed (if she had not agreed I
would have fired her!) to come.'

THIS EXTRACT FROM the Duchess of York's diary, dated 18 October 1992,
describes the occasion on which I first met Jane. As the date
suggests, the meeting occurred only 58 days after the traumatic
South of France photos. Since that day Sarah had remained in self-
imposed exile in Romenda Lodge, shunning any public appearance
and sequestering herself clandestinely with John Bryan. John
smuggled himself through the gates of Romenda, often hiding in the
boots of the series of anonymous-looking cars he rented each night
in order to return to his royal consort. Sarah described her situation
as analogous to the aftermath of a rape. She felt guilt, betrayal, anger,
self-loathing and fear of people. At this time John tried to convince
Sarah to publicly acknowledge her relationship with him, and even
to announce their engagement.

Prior to this débâcle Sarah had sold the rights to her second non-
fiction book on the life of Queen Victoria. The time had come for her
to begin a series of trips that would recreate the journeys Victoria had
taken throughout Europe. As the jacket of the completed book would
put it: 'The authors have immersed themselves in Queen Victoria's
library to reconstruct the journeys . . . they traced her in Rhineland
palaces and fortresses, and in forgotten castles deep in middle Europe.'

Sarah had decided that she was not willing to be escorted on these trips by John, so I was asked to accompany her on these frightening expeditions into a world that had seen her privacy so painfully exposed. She decided to take Jane along on these trips. Sarah often had troubled relationships with her staff and at this point Jane was in favour as a loyal and willing companion. As Sarah put it: 'Jane . . . whose loyalty and devotion knows no bounds.'

I waited in the baggage-claim area for BA flight 914 arriving in Frankfurt at 9.50 a.m. I had already met Sarah and Prince Andrew the previous February and had helped the Duke to select a home for her, but I had not yet met Jane. During the ensuing months, the couple had gone through a turbulent period. John Bryan was seen as a friend to both the Duke and Duchess, and Prince Andrew had trusted him.

Sarah and John had gone on a series of vacations together prior to their relationship being so sensationally exposed by the press. John was consistently warned that he was playing with fire. As I was later to learn, John assumed that Sarah would soon be his. He knew of her double divorce pact with Princess Diana, and he knew that her former lover Steve Wyatt was ensconcing himself in a safe lifestyle in America. All John needed to do was convince Sarah that he was both very rich and madly in love. In the aftermath of the photos he, too, was being punished. Beginning with this trip and continuing for the four years that remained of their romance, John was never to be Sarah's official escort again.

I recognised Sarah as she descended the escalator and looked over at her rather young and somewhat timid assistant. Only Jane walked beside her – the once obligatory bodyguards had been withdrawn by the palace and the retinue that had traditionally accompanied this royal duchess was reduced to a solitary dresser. 'Hello, ma'am. It's me, Allan,' I said tentatively, recognising that she was nervous and a little frightened.

'Oh, Starkie!' she exclaimed with relief. 'This is Jane Dunn-Butler.'

My diary from that day describes my first impression:

> One glance at Jane is really all one needs to know her: yet, I spent the subsequent days confirming that the impression was real. You see, Jane's eyes tell the story. They are filled

20

with sincerity, loyalty, and love. They shine with an inner honesty and devotion, clouded often and swiftly by fear and doubt when she believes she has displeased. There is a certain tentative quality about her when it comes to speaking of herself: almost as if to ask the listener if he really wants to hear, if he believes her life to be important enough to discuss with her. I am convinced that life has somehow injured her; yet, she seems to concentrate the force of her not inconsiderable emotional strength on serving her mistress.

It is funny now in retrospect to review my first reaction. As you might recall, I categorised Jane earlier as an empty vessel and it seems that I knew this at once by my description of her as someone you can know in 'just one glance' and as a person with a 'tentative quality'. That was Jane in 1992, long before her mimicked grand mannerisms would earn her the title of Lady Jane from the other members of Sarah's staff. In those early years Jane had been in Sarah's employ for four years, about half the time she would ultimately spend working for the Duchess. Those had been the 'royal years', the years in which Jane was kept distant from the Duchess, just one of a huge retinue. Those were the years in which Jane was to be treated purely as a servant and not yet as the confidante that she would become.

It is interesting here to note that Sarah traditionally had confusing relationships with servants. By this point she had already earned the wrath of the Duke of Edinburgh by greeting the royal servants by their Christian names and making some harmless small-talk. The enraged Duke commented with a look of disdain, 'I thought you had given up flirting with the servants ages ago.' Despite such august admonishments, Sarah continued to cross the line between employer and friend with her favourite servants. As this story progresses you will see that Sarah's servants *were* her closest friends. Those in favour would not only receive her most intimate confidences, but would even attend her private parties as guests.

Jane had not yet achieved the status of friend at this point in their relationship. Sarah had bonded with her personal secretary Jane Ambler and it was she who then shared Sarah's secret thoughts. At this point, Jane Ambler had to drop out of the royal scene for medical reasons and Jane Dunn-Butler was given her first real opportunity to penetrate into the Duchess's inner circle. This opportunity would create a new phase in Jane's life. She would be exposed to intimate insights of royal life and become privy to Sarah's thoughts. This trip was the beginning of an initially short-lived, but highly intoxicating period in which Jane was directly associated and deeply influenced by the force of the Duchess's personality. With Sarah's vacillating nature, relationships were generally tempestuous. There would be rejections and periods of increased acceptance, each bringing a distinct change in Jane's behaviour and ultimately a metamorphosis in her personality. No one could have predicted the extent of the change that Jane would begin to undergo, but the evolution was to commence on this very day in the early autumn of 1992.

Understanding that the Duchess was to be shorthanded and not accustomed to travelling light, I had decided to bring my own driver, a burly Turk named Ahmed, with a mini-van to transport the baggage. Also, I invited Anna Delnef, my private secretary, whom I planned on lending to the Duchess to act as secretary and interpreter. I made all the introductions then watched Ahmed struggle with an endless array of massive Louis Vuitton vintage cases that Sarah had borrowed from 'Anasha Weinberg, as . . . they looked a similar style to what QV would have with her back in 1845'.

We loaded the vehicles and began our trip to Coburg – the birthplace of Prince Albert. During the loading process Sarah had hardly uttered a sound, and Jane stood next to her smiling slightly and looking protective. I had instructed my driver to follow us in the van with the luggage and decided to drive Sarah in my own car. She sat next to me in the passenger seat while Anna and Jane occupied the back. Noticing the car phone, Sarah asked if she could call to tell John that she had arrived safely. After finishing the conversation she seemed a little more at ease and we began to make small-talk about the plans for the trip. 'I thought I would get you safely to Coburg, ma'am, and then I would return to Frankfurt tomorrow morning – but you can keep my driver and secretary for the duration of your trip.'

'Thank you, Starkie,' she said wearily.

We entered the autobahn and as I picked up speed I could feel the Duchess's mood begin to lift. Sarah's self-imposed exile of almost two months had finally been broken and she began to take heart. As she recalls in her diary of the time:

The black BMW sped off into the countryside of Germany –
it was a changeable day and the autobahn provided a speedier
route . . . Germany appeared immediately to be overwhelming
in its strength . . . I suddenly began to be aware that I was
away from GB – away from responsibilities, away from the
pressures of modern communications – i.e. the media – I
could indulge in being alone, so to speak, with people who
would not require me to be anything other than myself. I was
happy – content – a moment of peace cascaded through my
veins . . . I felt secure in the company of my new friends; they
did not judge me.

That car was to become her refuge for many trips, over many
months. Soon the conversations of each trip began to build up an
understanding of our various personalities, the crises that Sarah
faced, her fears and regrets and even a plan for the future. Jane
usually sat in the back and listened, or slept. At times I believe she
seemed to be sleeping when in actuality she was listening. Sarah
would reveal the most about herself and would probe for
information about John while the other two slept. As Sarah would
later describe these journeys: 'Travel has often been used as a
metaphor for growth and the path toward self-realisation. This trip
was no exception.'

Armed with the personal diaries of Queen Victoria, we headed
north towards the birthplace of Prince Albert. This was the
destination where the newly married royal couple were able to revisit
the magical places of Albert's youth, and where Victoria absorbed
every detail of Albert's childhood.

Despite the two highly documented romances in Sarah's life since
her marriage to Prince Andrew, I believe that she was still very much
in love with him (or at least desperately wanted to be) and tried to
relate to Victoria's great love for her prince. On the way to Coburg
Sarah mused in her diary:

I remembered back to my marriage and soon after – when I
was so excited when Andrew started to show me, with so
much pride, the magical places he remembered as a child. All
I wanted to do was engulf this man and his life, and all the
history of his full years. I was so passionately interested and

not a minute went by when I did not profess undying love for 'my jewel of a husband'. It seemed to me to be so comfortable to understand the passion QV had for Albert.

With Sarah drowned in these thoughts, we recognised that it would be best to remain quiet and so it was a pensive drive to Coburg.

We finally arrived at a quaint German inn where we would spend the first night. The hotel bore the impressive name of Schloss Neuhof ('*Schloss*' means 'castle' in German). The reception and dining-rooms were decorated with massive, gothic furnishings, the bedrooms plain but inoffensive. The owner was a very Teutonic and masculine-looking lady who seemed put off by the identity of her guest. Sarah typically travelled under several pseudonyms and so we were always greeted with some surprise on her arrival. The innkeeper really did have a negative attitude towards us. To make matters worse, we were next greeted by a woman whose demeanour made me reassess my initial negative appraisal of the innkeeper. Benita Stoney, our historian, came looming into the lobby, announcing in a soon-to-become-familiar, terse tone that we were very late and had no time to freshen up or have lunch. 'You will miss the light,' was her angry warning.

'Who is that woman?' I asked Jane. 'She helped Her Royal Highness with the last book on Osborne House,' she answered. 'So?' I asked, still incredulous that she could be so pushy. 'Her uncle runs the royal archives,' whispered Jane in a knowing and conspiratorial way. 'That is very important to Her Royal Highness.'

After depositing our luggage and grabbing a quick picnic lunch box, we went immediately to the first of two local castles, which were featured in Victoria's first visit to Albert's birthplace. The first was called Vestie, and was an interesting hodge-podge of various architectural styles spliced together over the centuries. We had engaged an excellent photographer named Robin Matthews to photograph the castles, which still stood since Victoria first visited them. He had been waiting for us at Vestie in a strange, dusty, dark barn that housed the 'sled museum'. It was here that the first photos for the book were to be taken. Robin was a young, vibrant man with a lot of charm and we immediately warmed to him. Standing in the shadows of the large hall was his very attractive assistant, Stephanie Hornett. She was a pixie-like beauty with short dark hair that stood straight up and beautiful grey eyes. She had a very smooth, angelic complexion that required virtually no make-up and firm, well-formed breasts that needed no support. Despite her almost childlike appearance, she met my gaze and seemed to take inventory of me, with a slight smile on her lips. I was immediately aware of her latent sexuality, just as I had been aware of Jane's innate sadness. In my diary I described Stephanie and her various conflicting descriptions of her life as: 'A lascivious little imp from Devon via Ethiopia, London, or Jamaica (depending on her mood).'

As I stared at Stephanie, I noticed that Jane was looking at me, studying my reaction and interaction with Stephanie. When I returned Jane's gaze she dropped her eyes and blushed. In those days it was her trademark reaction. We had all only just met, but the elements required for a painful triangle were already in place.

As Robin began the shoot, a horde of German tourists swarmed around us, having recognised the Duchess. Jane was quickly dispatched to disperse them and ran like a guard dog to bay at the tourists until they withdrew. The Duchess smiled at her and said proudly, 'Good girl, Jane – be a terrier!'

Next we went to a stately castle called Schloss Ehrenberg. It had been a favourite of Victoria's and she frequented it so often that an elevator had been installed just for her. It had long been plastered over. Behind the massive portrait-cluttered halls was a secret labyrinth of narrow corridors, entered through secret passageways. This is how the servants flitted like invisible creatures to silently service their masters. It underscored how different the relationship had been between aristocrat and servant a little over a century ago. They had lived in mirror worlds, as if they existed in different dimensions. I assume that Prince Philip still understood that world, and that is what he meant by admonishing the Duchess for her over-familiar ways.

'It reminds me of the palace,' said Jane. 'Do you spend a lot of time there?' I asked. 'I mean, in Buckingham Palace.' 'Yes, we have an office there, and the Duchess and the Duke still have rooms there – I used to live in the palace too . . . but . . .'

Before she could finish what I later learned was a kind of confession, we were interrupted. Jane would get a chance to finish her story and would do so in the fitting ambience of Buckingham Palace itself. I would have to wait two months to learn how she had come to live in a palace, and how she had come to leave it.

As the Duchess changed clothes, I played 'Greensleeves' on a piano that Prince Albert had once used. Jane sang along (in her original regional accent, as it still had not been eradicated to the point where she could sing in a refined manner) and Sarah came running out to join in. The Duchess had put on a stunning velvet dress and was wearing a choker necklace tightly around her throat. It was a band of gold with one large stone in the centre and had been a recent and somewhat extravagant gift from John. After the shoot, Jane took care of packing up the formal clothes and placing the jewellery in a small, locked box which she held to her breast like an infant child until we were able to secure it. I point this out because it was typical of Jane's protective behaviour to Sarah's wardrobe and jewellery. Ironically, Jane was first to be splashed across the headlines of the world's press not as the hunted fugitive, but as the 'gem of a helper' who lost the Duchess's jewels by placing them in the cargo hold of an areoplane in December of 1995. But we had many roads to travel before Jane was to encounter what Andy Warhol might have considered *both* of her 15 minutes of fame.

When we finished, we walked to the town square over a cobblestone street bracketed by the Rathaus (town hall) and public buildings. The Duchess seemed drawn to a particular path, as if she knew exactly where she was going. At one point she stopped and insisted on painting a particular street scene. Later she was to discover that Victoria had painted an almost identical watercolour of the same building, from precisely the same angle. It was the first of what was to become a pattern of coincidences that began to convince both Sarah and Jane that supernatural powers were at work, and that we were instruments of them.

It was getting late and we returned to the inn where Sarah and I decided to meet at 7.30 before the others joined us for dinner. When I came down at 7.00 Jane was there alone, seated in a rustic booth made of dark wood. She was apparently waiting for me. She knew that the Duchess was coming down shortly and clearly was trying to make an effort to get to know me quickly. It is strange, but until that time her appearance, whether or not she was physically attractive, had not made much of an impact on me. I knew that I liked her and somehow even felt sorry for her, but I had not noticed how she looked. She had put on some make-up before this meeting and had made an effort to look good, but there were things about her face that just seemed incongruous. In those days her hair was a dirty blonde, a little over shoulder length, but she wore it pulled back severely in an Alice-band. Her eyes were large and almost always sad, or at best serious. This often seemed at odds with a broad smile which somehow seemed out of place with such sad eyes. It gave one the impression that she was trying too hard – trying to please, and trying to *seem* pleased or happy. Her face was rather long and her jaw was very pronounced, as was her high forehead. Her head seemed so large that one did not at first even notice her body, which was very slender. I do not want to imply that she was unattractive – that would not be fair. To return to my former analogy, Jane seemed like a vessel filled with sadness and exuding melancholy and neediness. Were the same vessel filled with joy and self-assurance, it would have made a very different and more favourable impression. When one looked at Stephanie one thought of sex; when one looked at Jane, one felt protective and even a little depressed.

As I sat next to her, she smiled and I noticed that her canine teeth were long, sharp and a little distended. Combined with her other features it gave one the impression of addressing a shy and somewhat depressed vampire. 'The Duchess will be down soon,' she said nervously, as if to let me know that I need not talk to her for long.

'It has been a long day for the two of you, I bet,' I said, to make small-talk.

'Oh yes, we got up at five and it has been very tiring for Her Royal Highness.'

'It will be a busy few days,' I went on, 'but it will do the Duchess good to get away from England for a while.'

'Oh yes!' exclaimed Jane. 'It has been so hard for her and we – she is so grateful that you are helping her like this; she is very upset and frightened, and so brave to still make this trip.'

When she almost said 'we' instead of 'she', Jane's face had turned a bright red and she lowered her eyes in a gesture right out of *Jane Eyre*.

'I am happy to help. I was even thinking of remaining with her for the whole trip instead of returning tomorrow to Frankfurt.'

'Oh, that would be so kind!' she exclaimed. 'It would mean so much to her . . .'

There was something about Jane that I did not want to overly encourage. As I got the clear impression that it was she who wanted me to stay on for the duration, I decided it would be a good time to point out that I had a girlfriend.

'I have a lot of work to do back in Frankfurt,' I began. 'Also, I promised my girlfriend that I would only be gone for one night.'

'I see,' she said with her eyes clouding over quickly in hurt. 'Do you work with John?' she asked to disguise her reaction.

'Yes, we are partners in a construction business and our office is in Frankfurt,' I replied cheerfully.

'My father works in that field,' she said, as if she were searching for common ground.

'In London?' I asked, trying to be polite, for it was clear from her accent that her family could not have come from London.

'No,' she replied, shaking her head. 'Up north,' she added almost apologetically.

We did not have time for a long talk and I understood that there had been a hidden agenda – Sarah wanted an opinion about me and had sent Jane to do a little research. In those circumstances, I suppose, it was not odd that Jane did not mention she was married.

Sarah came down and sent Jane away with a brush of her hand and those mock-imperious, horse and hound phrases one could find so charming. 'Trot on, Jane.' Jane curtseyed and relocated to a table across the room, just within earshot. I learned that she was supposed to keep the other members of our team away from us until dinner, so that Sarah could concentrate on the task at hand. Sarah immediately began to turn on her charm. She was grateful, vulnerable and seemed to want to know everything about me – and John. 'Oh, Starkie, you have no idea how grateful I am for your help,' she began, with a warm Sarah smile. Let me tell you about those smiles. I am sick of hearing people say that she is not attractive or that she is common. The Duchess of York is extremely attractive and when she focuses her charm on a person he or she will invariably become her slave. Her smile is not just a function of her mouth – it is a co-ordinated combination of a mischievous flickering of her blue-grey eyes, a slight lowering of her head and a warm, knowing smile. It implies volumes. It makes subtle promises and, most of all, it appears that she has only just discovered how to really smile, and that it was reserved for you.

'My pleasure,' was about all I could squeeze out. I was transfixed by those eyes – and she knew it.

'You and John are very close. He thinks the world about you,' she continued.

'Well, he is pretty crazy about you too, ma'am,' I replied.

'The poor fellow has had a rough time in the last two months, but things will improve,' she said bravely.

'You both have,' I added.

'Tell me all about JB, Starkie. Tell me if I can trust him.'

Now, imagine that. I had only seen her three times in the previous eight months and never alone. We had begun this conversation ten minutes ago and already she was asking me to tell her the truth about my best friend, implying that she trusted me to do so.

And so I began to tell her a lot of things about John. I amazed myself at how honest I was. I told her about his abortive relationship with Lady Ogilvy, the daughter of the powerful press baron Lord Rothermere. I told her that John had trouble maintaining relationships and that they invariably ended in hatred, even giving examples. 'Several months ago he gave me a pair of squash sneakers and I knew that before they wore out we would not be on speaking terms.' Then I added hurriedly, 'But I go through shoes slowly – and I don't mean that the two of you will end on bad terms.' It was too late. I had given away too much. I will say two things about that first exchange. In all the years of shared confidences and betrayals in the complex relationships among Sarah, John and me, Sarah never told him my confession. She kept that trust. The second thing is that I still have those squash shoes, but have not spoken to John in four years. At any rate, without meaning to win her trust I succeeded in doing so. Later she would compare notes with Jane and the two of them would agree that I had passed their first test.

As we continued our discussion, members of the team began to hover near enough to our booth to be noticed. Jane succeeded at keeping them at bay, but was unable to stop the advance of the relentless Benita, who walked straight over and interrupted our conversation. The Duchess threw me one of her endearing looks, indicating that we would pretend to humour this intrusion, and we got up to join the others for dinner.

The innkeeper had set up a large table in a private dining-room just for us. Initially it was intended that Ahmed, Anna and Jane would eat in another room, but Sarah insisted that we all eat together. It was very democratic. The sense of camaraderie had already begun to form and, despite her fatigue, Sarah was funny and charming. Robin had an enormous arsenal of jokes and let loose with them almost immediately. Jane and Stephanie sat opposite me at either end of the table – it was awkward catching Stephanie's eye and at the same time feeling Jane's eyes upon me from the other corner.

We were all drinking pretty heavily and even Benita loosened up under the influence of the alcohol. After dinner someone suggested that we play conkers. The Teutonic innkeeper even joined in and instead of using a string returned with a rubber band, managing to turn the conker into an elastic projectile. At this point Sarah came to bid me goodnight. 'Will we see you before you leave tomorrow morning?' she asked, in a way that implied she already knew I would not be leaving. 'I think I can manage to stay with you for the rest of the trip,' I responded. She simply smiled and went off to bed.

I sensed that both Jane and Stephanie were trying to catch my attention and break off for a private conversation. Finally Stephanie went up to her room and I talked to Jane a little more; she thanked me for being kind to the Duchess and said how glad she was that I was staying. 'This is the first time I have seen her having fun in a long while,' she observed.

The group was breaking up and we walked up to the second floor, where we all had our separate rooms. Stephanie's room was next to the stairwell and I noticed that the door was ajar. Jane's room was next to mine. When we reached my door Jane stopped and turned towards me. It was a strange moment, as if we had just concluded a date and she expected to be kissed goodnight, or even invited in. 'Well, I will see you at breakfast tomorrow,' I said. She remained motionless for another instant, this time actually meeting my gaze. 'Goodnight,' she finally replied with a look of resignation.

I watched her walk towards her door, insert the large key in the lock and then place her hand on the doorknob. Funny – as I write I realise that that must be pretty much how she looked as she tied Thomas Cressman's doorknob shut with the cord of her bathrobe.

I looked over at her and again she met my gaze, her hand frozen on the knob of the door. 'Goodnight,' I said once more and, leaving her standing in the hall, entered my room.

I counted to 30, then opened the door a crack and peered out. She was gone. I flew down the stairs to beg the innkeeper for a fresh bottle of wine and two glasses. After explaining that it was against house rules, she provided me the items with a sly look — as if we were about to paint obscenities on the wall of a public building together.

Running up the steps I confirmed that Stephanie's door was still open, although the width of the opening had been reduced in size, almost like the closing treasure cave of Aladdin.

I knocked lightly and entered. Stephanie was seated on her bed waiting for me. She was wearing loose silk pyjamas with nothing underneath. We sat on the floor and quickly finished the bottle of wine, then I began to kiss her. She giggled and pulled her pyjama top over her head, without even taking the time to unfasten the buttons. Her breasts were perfectly shaped, as I had imagined. She was both aggressive and passionate and the night flew by. The next morning I realised that we were meant to meet for breakfast in less than an hour and quietly returned to my room.

The others had already started breakfast when I finally arrived. At the buffet table, Sarah gave me a very big smile and in a low, deep voice said, 'Didn't sleep much last night, uh, Starkie.' It was a statement, not a question, and simultaneously implied a sense of admiration, feigned surprise and pride at possessing the information. It brought me to the point of paranoia. It was several weeks later before Sarah admitted that Jane had told her she had overheard sounds in the night. Yet somehow that explanation still did not seem to answer the question of how Jane *knew* I had been sleeping with Stephanie. Later, as the situation got more severe, I was to learn what Jane did with *her* nights. For her part, Jane greeted me that morning with a look of hurt. She literally seemed disappointed in me. I smiled at her and said 'Good morning' as cheerfully as I could. She made a barely audible reply and walked away.

CHAPTER THREE

WUTHERING HEIGHTS

AFTER BREAKFAST WE DROVE to 'our dearest Rosenau'. Yes, the spell of Victoria's words was beginning to have a noticeable affect; Rosenau, the birthplace of Albert, was Victoria's greatest shrine to her undying love. On the drive to Rosenau Sarah read Victoria's diaries out loud amid the purring of Jane and Anna at the romantic spots.

Rosenau sits on a small, grassy hill. Its neo-gothic appearance is reminiscent of the home of Sir Walter Raleigh and it is a peaceful, calm and very human dwelling. Sarah stood at the foot of the hill and painted the castle in a watercolour that so closely resembled Victoria's style that it was truly uncanny. Albert had grown up in a loft-like room on the top floor and there were still holes in the wall from his fencing foil. The magic of the Victorian love affair seemed still very much alive in that room. In fact, the small castle of Rosenau still seemed vibrantly alive with the love of Victoria and Albert. Sarah and Jane appeared to be very moved by the ambience and I recorded their feelings in my diary. The Duchess felt that it captured the mood, and used the passage in our final book: 'The clearest ghost in the Rosenau is the still-powerful trace of the unqualified love that she lavished on Albert. It is a happy place.'

Despite the pleasant atmosphere earlier in the day, by the end of the morning, as we were completing our visit, Sarah simply stopped talking to anyone but Jane. She barely answered me when I posed direct questions. I immediately sought out Jane (a pattern I would follow for many years to come) to find out what was wrong. She had apparently recovered from her anger towards me and seemed pleased that I sought her out. 'Oh, Allan, I am sure it has nothing to do with you,' she said consolingly.

'It must – she won't even speak to me,' I insisted.

'She is under a lot of pressure right now, that is all,' was Jane's response. But in a pattern that would also be often repeated, Jane went directly to Sarah to report that I was concerned. Within a few minutes the Duchess came to me with a troubled look on her face. She never acknowledged that Jane had tipped her off and generally she would not. I think it made her happy to use Jane as a spy and let others believe that Sarah was just very perceptive or empathetic. 'Starkie, Starkie, I am so very happy you are here and everything is fine. I am just so upset with Benita – it has nothing to do with you!' she exploded.

'Why?' was all I had time to ask.

'She has agreed to do another book on Victoria and she said that she wants to do it alone! I put her on the map. It's not fair. It is very sad indeed.' Jane looked on as if to say 'I told you it had nothing to do with you', a faint smile on her lips. She was glad to have done me a favour and it showed.

We drove to a tree that Victoria had planted 120 years ago, then on to a small private castle which had been almost obliterated during the war by bombs. There was very little left of the original structure, but by some miracle a single pane of glass had survived the bombing. Scratched upon it with a diamond were the signatures of three of Victoria's grandchildren: 'Victoria, Irene, Alix'. Alix would grow up to be Alexandra, the last Tsarina of Russia. She would be executed in 1917 by the Bolsheviks; but when she scratched her name on that pane of glass, she was just a playful little girl. Somehow those fragile signatures captured on crystal had survived for over a hundred years and two world wars. Jane and I stared at the glass in amazement.

'It makes me think of Beatrice and Eugenie,' said Jane quietly.

We were very aware that Sarah's husband and children were direct descendants of Victoria; therefore, they were related to the three little princesses who had playfully autographed this window pane. It was an eerie feeling. I mean, those girls were actually *relatives* of Sarah's children! The realisation of our proximity to family history seemed to impact on Jane.

'Do you like children?' she asked.

'Most of the time,' I replied, thinking of the poorly behaved children I had so often seen.

'I would love to have a child,' continued Jane as if she had not even heard my answer. She was lost in her dreams. Perhaps she was imagining bearing a playful little princess of her own. In any case, she exuded a pitiful sense of longing. It was so pronounced that I wondered if she was barren and mourning her inability to be a mother.

While having tea with the owner of the castle, Sarah excused herself to make a call. When she returned her face was dark and her mood blacker. The omniscient Jane explained: 'She called Her Majesty the Queen and I guess it did not go well. I believe Her Majesty is going to be in Germany and Her Royal Highness was hoping that they might be able to see one another.'

We drove towards the Rhine River, surrounded by steep hills which are populated by ancient castles that belonged to the robber barons who extracted tolls from the ships which once passed through the mighty river. It is a stunning piece of countryside and after a while the Duchess came out of her depression.

'Starkie,' she began. 'Those people with whom we had tea were so nice to me.'

'Yes,' I agreed, 'they certainly were.'

'Were they nice,' she went on, 'because I am HRH the Duchess of York, or just because I am me?'

This was not an easy question to answer tactfully. We had been given carte blanche to enter and photograph both public and private castles, which no ordinary tourist could hope to see. We had been treated royally and the reason was obvious.

'Well,' I ventured, 'I think that your title does open doors for us, but if you lost it I am sure that people would still like you.'

'I will never lose it!' she exploded. 'I will always be a princess of the British empire.' I looked in the rear-view mirror and saw Jane stiffen with a look of terror, so I dropped the issue and simply smiled at my companion.

We arrived at a small hotel called the Rhine Villa and had a few minutes before dinner. I decided to use the time to buy gifts for Beatrice and Eugenie. Although I had not yet met the little princesses, I had heard so much about them from both John and Sarah that I wanted to make sure they would have souvenirs from

Germany. I was gone for no more than 20 minutes, but Sarah had already been informed of my absence by Jane and called my room the moment I returned. 'Out for a little stroll, Starkie?' she asked. 'Well, meet me downstairs and let us continue our talk.'

Before we could really begin, Benita stormed over and demanded an audience with the Duchess. Some time later an exhausted Sarah returned and we all met for dinner. We were tired and there were few jokes, and no conkers. Jane eyed me warily through dinner, watching my interaction with Stephanie. I was even more careful and quiet that night and the next morning I could tell that Jane was not certain whether I had been with Stephanie or not. She was cheerful and talkative. But it was on this day that I would finally get a true insight into the mind of Jane Dunn-Butler.

We drove to the ferry and crossed the Rhine. On the other side, we continued to an old stone castle high on a hill, parked in front of it and began an ascent up the narrow path to the peak of the hill. The path climbed, curved and doubled over leading us to the summit, past the vineyards. On the top stood a lone stone castle tower. Jane walked alongside me, following the lead of the Duchess. It was a grey, dismal day with a light mist of rain falling on us as we walked.

From this high and windy vantage point, the Rhine Valley stretched out beneath us. The powerful river lay far below, flexing itself with unfaltering strength. The mountaintops bordering the valley were crowned with evergreens cutting a jagged horizon against the stormy grey sky. Below, tree-lined vineyards cascaded down to the water's edge, disturbed only by a toy railway line built too close to the road. Our hilltop was fairly flat, interrupted only by a strange rock formation protruding from the earth in overlapping slabs of grey granite. To the right of us stood a deserted tower, massive and silent, staring at us through two lifeless windows. The parapets were overgrown and reclaimed by nature. Here one could see both the conflict and the harmony of nature and man. The mountains had been stripped of their natural foliage and ordered into neat rows of cultured vines, yet at the same time nature was silently and patiently reclaiming the stone tower, returning it to its elemental origins.

The foreboding grey skies gathered their clouds for yet another of the countless storms that have pounded those cliffs since they emerged from the earth as molten lava millions of years ago. The river pumps quietly and steadily, ignorant of the gazes of countless generations of humankind that have looked upon it. Standing on that hilltop, it is easy to be overwhelmed by our seeming insignificance. Jane was as moved as I was. She simply gazed at the river, tears beginning to well in her eyes. Her left hand reached automatically into the pocket of her fur-collared overcoat and she produced a crumpled tissue and slowly drew it to her nose. Then, with a gesture that I would later regard as one of the few things truly typical of Jane, she blew her nose without making the slightest sound.

Then the Duchess sat on that strange rock formation with the wind blowing her red hair, her heart beating life into the cold stone. As if she were a catalyst, the dark rainclouds parted and a single pure ray of the sun poured down upon us, like a spotlight from heaven. I was dumbstruck by the visual power of the scene and was able for the brief moment that it lasted to photograph first Sarah and then Jane, caught in that one ray of brilliant, cleansing light. I was unable to put what we had just experienced into words. Only Jane could do that. '*Wuthering Heights*,' she whispered.

That was it – she had caught it. It was similar to the haunting feelings that Heathcliff and Cathy shared on the heights of Penistone Crag, which their imaginations had turned into their own castle, their own world.

'Yes, Jane, that's it . . . how could you know that?' I asked with something between enormous respect and fear. 'What is that to you, Jane? Do you have your Heathcliff? Have you lost him? Is that your hurt, is that what has made you this way?'

'Maybe it's worse if you have not yet found Heathcliff,' she responded with moist eyes. She stared at me, then silently began to descend the hill, leaving the Duchess still seated on that outcropping. As we looked back over our shoulders, we saw she was sobbing so forcefully that her whole body shook.

I felt a profound closeness to Jane at that moment and wanted to know more about her. 'Who hurt you so much?' I asked suddenly.

She did not seem at all surprised by the question and simply answered, 'Maybe I will tell you one day.'

'Do you have someone in your life now, Jane?' I asked as we began the long walk downhill.

'Yes, I am married,' she said in a tone that sounded like an apology.

I must admit that I was utterly shocked by this answer. Jane's interest in me had seemed so clear that it had never occurred to me that she might be married, or even seriously involved. Now, after watching her reaction to *Wuthering Heights*, I found it difficult to reconcile her sense of longing and sadness with anything resembling a happy marriage.

'Was he ever Heathcliff to you?'

She smiled a thin, sad grin, then shook her head emphatically.

'Tell me about him,' I asked.

'Well, there is not very much to say.'

'What does he do?' I continued, hoping to get her to open up.

'Computers, he works with computers for IBM, but he is not doing too well, I don't think he's very ambitious.'

'Are you ambitious, Jane?' I asked.

She looked at me without saying a word, just gave me a hard stare which told me she *was* ambitious, but in a way she felt I might not understand. And so she said nothing at all.

'Have you been married long?' I continued.

'Two years,' she answered impatiently, as if the questions were beginning to annoy her. 'His father was an officer and he is very nice, but . . . I don't . . . I don't . . .' She interrupted this apparently difficult line of conversation with a request for me to tell her about my girlfriend. 'Well, she is very beautiful,' I said. 'She is half-Norwegian . . .' Before I could finish the sentence, she jumped in and said, 'Oh, so am I!' By the time we reached this point in our first truly personal conversation, Sarah had caught up with us and together we continued down the hill.

When the emotions calmed we would discuss *Wuthering Heights*. It would become a symbol of the little group's relationships with one another and the world, and for Jane especially the hope that somehow she would find the all-consuming, undying love that she sought. Jane and I would often refer to the book and sometimes I would revisit the hill and sit on the same rock outcropping. Sarah, always fond of nicknames and abbreviations, would ultimately come to call it simply 'the Rock'. She made me a beautiful photo collage of the three of us with the inscription 'I will always remember the feelings we all had on the Rock.' But for Jane and me, it was always *Wuthering Heights*. It created a great bond between us. For me the bond represented a sense of understanding, an affection that survived through the myriad incarnations of Jane's personality. Even now, I cannot help but admit to a strong residual fondness for the girl I first knew on the Rock. But for Jane it meant much more. From that moment, and for a long time, Jane believed that I belonged to her.

After our excursion to the Rock we crossed over the Rhine and drove back to our hotel. The three of us were physically exhausted after the experience on the hill and, in my case, the two nights with Stephanie. Nevertheless, the entire group was eager to have a fun evening, as it was the last night of the first trip. We ate together as a group and after dinner Sarah decided that we should play party games. The first game we chose was a form of 'Charades'. I believe it is well known in England, but I had never encountered it before. A member of the group is sent out of the room and the remaining people chose either an adjective or adverb that ends in 'ly', such as aggressively, or forcefully. The selected person returns and then creates a scenario in which selected members of the group must act out a scene in the manner of the word.

The reason I remember that game so well is because it revealed so much about Jane's character. I think it is often surprising how ostensibly introverted people will behave when given the opportunity to act like someone else. Jane was a prime example. Robin was the first contestant and when he returned to the room he selected Jane and me. 'Jane,' he announced, 'pretend that Allan is a car and drive him in the manner of the word.' The word was 'aggressively' and she played it to the hilt. She slammed my doors with rage, switched my gears with anger, pounded on my back to honk the horn with a convincing fury and in no time at all Robin had guessed the word. I saw Jane differently after that. Earlier that day I had seen that she was a volcano of unfulfilled passion ready to explode. Then, two hours later, I witnessed the degree of rage which seemed to be a component of her passion. I decided to be extra careful that night and virtually crawled into Stephanie's room.

For the remainder of the trip Jane followed me constantly. The first opportunity that we had to be alone, she asked, 'Did you read *Wuthering Heights* or just see the movie?'

'Both,' I replied, 'and it was one of the few times I thought that a screenplay writer had improved upon the original.'

She brightened up at this and asked me what I meant. I remember the exchange very well because it was the final day of our first trip and we were in a very elegant castle called Bruhl. Sarah had been walking ahead of us and apparently needed Jane for something and turned around, annoyed to find Jane deep in conversation with me.

What I was telling her was that in Brontë's original, the mourning Heathcliff stands over the lifeless body of Cathy and says, 'I cannot live without my life, I cannot live without my soul.' But in the revised film version, he says, 'I cannot live without my life, I cannot *die* without my soul,' which I felt was more poignant in depicting the horrible state of empty limbo in which he was trapped. He was caught in a state of intense suffering and loneliness, in which even the escape of death was to be denied him.

She listened silently and her eyes filled with tears. She was only able to nod her head vigorously and say, 'Yes, I think so too . . . that would be much more terrible.'

Looking back on her reaction in light of what I now know – I think I can begin to understand her state of mind shortly after she killed Thomas. During her nightmarish flight to Cornwall she expressed a similar state of hopelessness to Lucinda Sharp. Jane wanted so desperately to die; yet, somehow was unable to do so. She was caught in the same horrible limbo that had terrified her in *Wuthering Heights* – trapped by the power of a lost love that prevented her both from living and from dying.

Just then Sarah emerged and castigated Jane for not being available when she needed her. It was odd to watch such an exchange. It was like a slap in the face – because for the very first time I thought that I had seen the real face of Jane Dunn-Butler.

The end of the first trip was very sad. Sarah had to return to an England that felt hostile, and Jane . . . well, Jane was not going to return to Heathcliff. In the airport Sarah wrote a little note to me then hugged me. I promised that I would always be her escort and that she need never travel again without me. And with very few exceptions I kept that promise for the next four years. Jane stared into my eyes then gave me a hug – again her eyes filling with tears. 'You know how I feel,' was all she could say.

I drove back home, my planned one-night journey having turned into more than I had anticipated. I was intrigued by Sarah and confused and saddened by Jane. When I returned home I found this message from Sarah on my answering machine:

Hello Allan, Allan, why aren't you picking up the phone you naughty, naughty boy? You're out playing conkers, aye. Hmmm . . . Think you could be . . . hope you got home safely and you are just completely wonderful . . . and thank you so much for giving me three magical days. And where the fuck are you? Why aren't you bugging me? Where are you? You should be here now! NOW! More rotwein Starkie now! Your girlfriend is going to think I am completely batty . . .

The next day a gift-wrapped box arrived filled with conkers couriered over from a London florist. That was Sarah's style. It was to be three weeks until the next research trip, but I received an invitation to come to England the moment I returned from a business trip to Moscow. Sarah asked me if I would use the time to write a diary of the trip.

CHAPTER FOUR

SEXUAL DEMANDS

EVEN PRIOR TO the South of France photos Prince Andrew needed a temporary home for his estranged wife. An extremely decent, fair and elegant person, the Prince was still trusting of John's good intentions. As a result, His Royal Highness invited John and me to have lunch with him at Sunninghill Park to discuss where to house Sarah and the two princesses.

Even in 1992 Sunninghill Park had an air of being incomplete. It simply did not feel like a home. The architecture was cold and impersonal and its ranch-like appearance led to its nickname of 'South York'. The interior designer had advised against the use of temporary fixtures until the ideal item could be found, so as a result a naked light bulb would be hanging in the sitting room until the perfect chandelier could be located. My favourite feature was a small alcove off the entrance foyer. In it hung the head of a buffalo and beneath that rested a knight's helmet. I thought it summarised Sarah's romantic dilemma.

Prince Andrew took us to a small, empty hunting lodge on the grounds of Windsor Great Park to ask our opinion on his having it renovated for Sarah and their daughters. It was too small and in poor condition and would probably have cost too much to renovate. Even then it might still have been inappropriate. The Queen had agreed to pay for the renovation and that was a pretty compelling factor to try to make the plan work, but there were too many drawbacks. For example, the property would have required a massive fence to prevent anyone travelling through the park from peeking in on the exiled royals. In the end, a rental property was decided on. John and I located and slightly renovated a mock Tudor home called Romenda Lodge. This was to be my first visit to the home since Sarah and the children had occupied it.

The taxi stopped at the black iron fence and the driver pressed the buzzer. The gates slowly swung open and two guards appeared to motion us in. Although Sarah was no longer given bodyguard protection, the two princesses would continue to receive the privilege. So, oddly, Sarah was well protected when she was in the presence of her daughters, but all alone when she travelled without them – not to discount the fearless qualities of Jane. Lurking behind the tall trees that lined the driveway were more guards, walkie-talkies in hand, silently looking on. For now they were just faceless strangers with guns.

The Duchess opened the door herself and hugged me. 'Oh, Starkie, I am so glad you could come!' she exclaimed and led me into her home. She had done a fantastic job in turning a house with little personality into a warm home – and she had done so with very few resources.

Let me describe the home. The house itself was rectangular and built in mock-Tudor style, that is to say, the façade was brick with exposed wooden beams. The main part of the house consisted of two floors with a small finished attic, in which the nanny lived. On the ground floor, a hallway ran the length of the building, ending in French doors which opened onto the garden behind the house. To the right of the entrance hallway was a room that was used as both study and sitting-room and to the left was the dining-room, which we used at times as a conference room. Next to the dining-room was a small nursery and adjacent to that was the kitchen. The top floor had six bedrooms and two bathrooms. The garden was fairly large and featured a pool house, which enclosed an indoor pool. In the back of the garden were a swing and a small wooden playhouse for the children. The garage was used as a base for the bodyguards, and eventually the small apartment above it would be furnished for the butler.

Escorting me into her study, Sarah announced that she had a surprise. Upon entering, I found Jane waiting inside and at first thought that she was meant to be my surprise. John strolled into the room, popping candies in his mouth and walking in his stockinged feet to show how casual he could be when 'at home'. The surprise turned out to be a treasure hunt. Sarah and Jane had hidden a number of gifts for John and me in the study. As we walked about they would yell 'warm' or 'cold'. We fumbled around recovering neckties and toiletries, and even a pair of red underpants adorned with cherubs.

I was then introduced to Sarah's daughters. It is odd now to look back at those little girls and the photos I still have of them, taken over the following four years. I knew even then and was aware throughout the following years that one day they would be strange faces to me, on the cover of international gossip magazines. There was something fatalistic about our whole inner group that implied the impossibility of sustaining those intimacies. Perhaps the awareness of the temporal nature of these delicate relationships allowed me to enjoy the period more – and to take an active interest in recording those events.

I must say that Jane shared a very warm relationship with the little princesses. They had already experienced a change of nannies and so Jane was a stabilising influence in their lives. She paid special attention to Beatrice and one could see a strong bond of affection between them. After the treasure hunt Jane watched a Walt Disney video with Beatrice and Eugenie and helped get them ready for tea.

We had tea in the dining-room and both girls jumped on their chairs and clapped their little hands together in prayer as they said: 'Dear God, thank you for our lovely tea. Can we get down now Mummy, please?' Jane stood up during this cute ritual and then, after ensuring that they had adequate supplies of Ribena, left the room. It was odd to watch the fine line that Jane walked at that time. This was the first opportunity I had been offered to watch Jane's interaction with Sarah in her role purely as a servant in her domestic surroundings. During our trips Jane would be allowed to eat with us and would often be included in very personal discussions, but here at Romenda Lodge, Jane was clearly regarded as just another servant, and it would have seemed terribly incongruous had she attempted to join us for tea. Her tentative and confusing status made me feel sorry for her, and I would watch the disparity in her treatment grow more confusing over the coming years.

As the cook cleared the table in preparation for our meeting, which would be held in the dining-room, I sought out Jane. She was in the garden watching Beatrice dangle from the bar of the swing. 'Oh, Allan, it is so good to see you again,' she said, with a big smile which exposed those prominent canine teeth that always gave me a fright.

'I am happy to see you too,' I replied, and realised that I genuinely meant it. We had undeniably shared something on the Rock along the Rhine, and the bond it forged was still very apparent.

After the treasure hunt and charming introductions to the little princesses the main reason for my invitation became clear. Sarah had already come to trust my judgement and John relied on me implicitly. As a result they wanted me to help them plan a course for Sarah's transition, to help her with her plans and projects, and to mediate the complex issues involved in her personal relationship with John. It was now 29 October 1992 and Sarah had reached a major crossroads in her life. She still had the chance to return to Prince Andrew – or she could expedite a divorce (as the Queen seemed to favour) and try to redefine herself through her charity and business enterprises. The difficulty she faced was that all these issues were combined in her mind. She was not sure that she really wanted to leave Andrew, yet she did not want to lose John, or her newly acquired freedom. She needed money, but was afraid to earn it in ways that might soil her royal image. As a result she sulked and suffered and was frightened most of the time. Jane was often at her side and would listen to the flow of misery, but seemed unable to assist her in any way. I think that the Duchess was very aware of Jane's limitations and of John's personal interests, and so she decided to give me a try. 'Starkie – run my life,' is how she put it.

During the Great Depression in the United States Franklin Delano Roosevelt initiated a series of calming radio broadcasts he called 'Fireside Chats'. I felt that instead of frightening the already terrified Duchess with elaborate staff meetings or 'business plans' (as John had intended), we initiate bi-monthly meetings where all issues could be calmly addressed among friends. I called these meetings 'Fireside Chats', and for the next four years they formed the framework for Sarah's life. There would be many successful chats and many very horrible confrontational ones. Today's was the first.

As the Fireside Chats evolved into larger and more complex issues, lawyers and accountants would become active participants, but today the attendees consisted of the Duchess, John, Jane and me.

Jane was there primarily to take notes for Sarah but she occasionally participated in the discussions.

Our first chat was structured around the creation of a set of criteria that could be used to select appropriate business projects without diluting Sarah's royal mystique. We came up with a list of ultra-restrictive parameters which eliminated virtually every prospective business opportunity that Sarah had been offered. This was precisely what John wanted. Ultimately we argued that only Greta Garbo and Jackie Onassis had managed to retain their iconic international repute. They had done so, we suggested, by minimising their exposure to the public. And so we tried to turn the Duchess into a Garbo-esque recluse.

After the meeting we had dinner at about eight and were all exhausted; nevertheless, we talked until one in the morning. Sarah let loose with royal stories either to impress me or as a catharsis. She spoke of Princess Diana, Princess Anne, Lord Mountbatten, and of the 'rules of the firm' as taught to her by the Duke of Edinburgh. My head was spinning by the time I was able to crawl to bed. I felt as if I'd had every ounce of energy drained from me. I was safe to sleep in the guest room without risk of any nocturnal visits from Jane as she did not live with the Duchess and had left after the chat.

I returned to Germany early the next morning and as I left I handed Sarah the diary I had written of our first trip. That was when the trouble with Jane really began. Sarah spent the next week, until the second trip, in bed. She was worn out and suffered from terrible migraines. She left my diary on her table and Jane had the opportunity to read it. As you may recall from the excerpts regarding Jane, I was not unkind in my initial impressions. Jane took my statement as nothing less than a confession of love. She barraged the Duchess with questions about me, to the point where Sarah complained to John that something needed to be done.

John promptly called me to say, 'Sarah loved your diary and wants to take large parts out of it and use them directly in the book.'

'That's great, John,' I replied, and waited, because John only led with compliments when he had something else to say.

'But you know where you made a big hit?' he asked tauntingly. 'With Jane!' He continued impervious to the fact that I had not been given time to answer. 'She is absolutely crazy about you and is bugging Sarah all the time with questions.'

'She is a very nice girl, John, and I like her a lot too,' I responded.

'Great, then fuck her next week. I bet she will be wild – you know, the quiet type. Boy, I bet she will tear you apart,' was John's assessment and recommendation.

Incidentally, John had a good instinct about this type of thing. His personal exploits were so great that we once tried to make a calculation of the number of conquests he boasted and ultimately were forced to settle with a statistical guess. Prior to my becoming his friend, John's best friends were Whitney Tower of the wealthy and socially prominent Tower family, and Mick Jagger. It was under the tutelage of Mick that John learned many of his most successful pick-up techniques. He even applied these rules to his business dealings, for he found them universally applicable.

John's favourite line, apparently a 'Jagger-ism', was 'go for the "no" quickly'. This cryptic line has its origin from the experiences John had undergone while going out with Mick. The clubs and restaurants that they frequented together generally cordoned off the table at which they sat, thus protecting them from over-zealous fans. Mick would allow John to make a selection from behind the velvet rope and the young lady would be permitted to join them. Ironically, many of them ultimately rejected John after Mick's departure. Mick taught John two essential rules:

1. Make the deal before you leave the table.
2. Go for the 'no' quickly.

What these professorial lines actually mean is simply: if a lady is going to refuse a one-night stand, she will do so regardless of how much time you invest in begging, getting to know her, or listening to her problems. She is as likely to say 'no' immediately as she will be after you have spent the evening with her; therefore, it is imperative that you pose the question quickly and see if the intent is a 'no'. If she does not refuse then make the 'deal' (proposition) concrete prior to leaving the (negotiating) table.

Armed with these words of advice, John was unstoppable. Naturally, John's success had elevated these rules into an almost religious significance in his set of priorities. So, with great respect, he again uttered them to me. 'Allan, the very first night in Milan, make the deal,' he said, now with a relished sense of authority.

'But, John,' I pleaded, 'I don't want to . . .'

My statement left him speechless. There was pure silence on the other end. For those who know John Bryan, that is a phenomenon.

'Huh,' he finally uttered in a muted, guttural whisper, as if he had been kicked in the stomach by his best friend. Then, 'Why not?'

'John, she is too needy. She would take it way too seriously.'

'Exactly!' he exploded. 'That is just why you have to do it.'

'But I will never get rid of her,' I protested.

'No, you idiot,' he went on, 'that is the only way to get rid of her. You have to fuck her then treat her like absolute shit, that is how she will get you out of her system.' Now he paused. The master had spoken and he wished to enjoy the full impact of his wisdom.

'I don't know,' I said thoughtfully. 'I am not so sure that I would get rid of her that way.'

'Give it a try,' was his final word on the matter, and he quickly changed the subject.

But I was not willing to be so cavalier about Jane. Even with Sarah's reinforcement of John's suggestion, I felt a strong aversion to encouraging Jane – and a sense of protectiveness towards her. It seems hard to believe that my successors in the men that would win Jane's future affections did not notice her strange sense of neediness and obsessiveness. Perhaps it was clearer to me in 1992 because Jane had not yet altered herself into a flamboyant and provocative copy of her mistress. Maybe in her future femme fatale persona, the pathetic, plaintive nature of her need would be less evident.

At any rate, I was not willing to tempt fate either for a quick fling or as a remedy to love-sickness.

CHAPTER FIVE

THE NIGHT STALKER

THE NEXT TRIP was to Italy and France, where Victoria travelled regularly. I flew to Milan airport, where I rented a car, and along with my secretary awaited the arrival of the Duchess and Jane. Their plane was delayed and they both looked tired but happy to see me. Sarah ran over and hugged me and, as I looked over her shoulder, I saw Jane staring at me with very apparent affection. 'Your brother wants you to call him – *now*, Starkie!' announced the Duchess. Sarah loved to create code names for everyone and John was given a large assortment of them. In 1992 Otto was the name of choice (in honour of Carl Otto Pohl, the former Bundesbank president, but that is another story). If you look at the dedication of her third Budgie book it is dedicated to 'Otto'. But she referred to John as 'your brother' to me, and she was either 'your Aunt Sally' or 'your sick Aunt' depending on her degree of depression.

'Can't he wait until we get to the hotel?'

'No, Starkie. It is very important – you just won a big business deal and he is very excited.'

So we fumbled around with the Italian pay-phone system and managed to exchange enough coins to call London. I made the call from the booth next to the luggage-retrieval area, with Sarah standing close enough to overhear. Jane and Anna waited by the bags, out of earshot.

'Hello, John. We are here in the airport and they just arrived. I hear that Rostock [the name of the project] is a done deal.'

'Yeah, yeah,' he responded, 'but what I wanted to tell you was don't forget to fuck Jane tonight.'

'You mean I had to call you from the airport to hear that again?' I said angrily.

'This is serious! I am not kidding, man. She has it bad for you and you had better fuck her. I discussed this with Sarah, and she will talk to you about it too.'

The Duchess had been close enough to hear the exchange and had broken into a mischievous grin. I hung up and we began the long drive to the lake district of northern Italy.

It was already dark and the drive along the autostrada was winding and precarious. The ground was blanketed in a seeping fog that would have made navigation difficult even during the day. Sarah was reading the map while speaking at the same time and was unable to concentrate. We almost drove off the road twice. I look back now and wonder: if I had smashed up my car on that dark road in Italy, how many conspiracy theories would have been devised to explain the death of the Duchess of York?

But on this crisp, foggy evening in November 1992 Sarah made it to Lago Maggiore without injury. As usual, our team was awaiting us in a state of polite starvation. We dropped off our bags and went straight to the dining-room, where we greeted Benita, Robin and Stephanie. I shook their hands, saving Stephanie for last, and as we grasped hands she smiled and simply would not let go. Jane inched up behind me and glared at Stephanie then sat next to her at the table, directly across from me.

As we discussed the days ahead and wolfed down our meal I could feel two feet running themselves along my respective legs. I wondered how long it would take before they collided and what the result would be. During the last trip Sarah had been fond of saying 'Silly not to' when being offered either dessert or a drink. Now I noticed that both Stephanie and Jane had adopted this phrase – and, indeed, nobody refused the steady flow of wine that we were offered.

The hotel featured a bowling alley, a strange thing for any hotel in Europe. So, we decided to go bowling after dinner, which was not exactly what I had on the agenda. As we walked down the long hallway to the bowling alley in that large, almost vacant hotel, we passed an indoor pool which seemed to appear out of nowhere. It was heated and fog was rising from it and steaming up the windows of the room. The thick ground covering of fog outside turned the grounds into an eerie landscape, and here indoors the same thick fog seemed to be seeping out of the pool as if it were a witches' cauldron. Benita's personality was at its best under the influence of alcohol and she began giggling, ran over to the steamed windows and traced a caricature of Queen Victoria on the glass. I could not believe it. I was convinced that Benita held Victoria in such reverence that any form of humour would be considered pure sacrilege. Yet soon the large head with a receding chin and tiny crown was placed upon a bulging body, as Benita shrieked with laughter.

We proceeded to the bowling alley, where I again faced the question of how to separate the two women. Stephanie had leaned against me with those perfect breasts rubbing against my chest and whispered, 'Why are you being so distant? I can't take it any longer! Let's take off our clothes and go swimming in that pool – now!' I had not briefed Steph on the recent developments with Jane and simply said, 'Certain people are aware of our relationship.'

'So?' she exclaimed.

Of course, she was right. Yet, I had such a strong intuition that we were in a precarious situation that I finally said, 'I'll explain it when we are alone,' not realising that what would happen that night would give Stephanie her own ample explanation.

What I did not tell Stephanie until later was that I had detected evidence that others were already trying to influence our situation. My secretary Anna had been made responsible for room arrangements in the various hotels along the way. Two days prior to this trip, we had received a call from Sarah's office saying that Benita was concerned that our trips were going over budget and was happy to share a room with Stephanie. We managed to avoid allowing Benita to make such a noble sacrifice, assuming that the request had really originated from her in the first place.

After the game we returned through that labyrinthine corridor towards the lobby, again passing the pool. I noticed that both Stephanie and Jane had stopped, so I said, 'Should we just skinny dip together?' Even Benita seemed intrigued by the suggestion, but to my relief she continued walking forward. For a few seconds I thought I might have accidentally hit on the most equitable way of managing the two ladies, but again I felt an intangible fear.

During the bowling game and now as we prepared to separate for the evening, Jane kept trying to catch my attention. I did my best to avoid being alone with her, but just as we approached the elevator she said, 'Allan, I must speak to you alone.'

'I am very tired, Jane,' I answered. 'Can't it wait until tomorrow?'

'No,' she whispered.

By this time the elevator had stopped on my floor and I simply walked out, saying, 'I promise to talk to you tomorrow.' As the door closed, she stood rigidly in the elevator cab with her face set in grim determination. I went to my room to see if the luggage had made its way there without me. As I was leaving I heard the phone ring, but left it unanswered.

Stephanie was already undressed and waiting for me with an impish smile on her face as I opened her unlocked door. 'What took you so long?' she teased. In the four steps it took to reach her bed I managed to undress completely, but as I jumped into her bed she stuck out her hand as if to stop me. 'If you plan on any of that you had better greet me with a little more than a handshake when you see me next,' she announced with a smile, but an apparent sense of annoyance.

'Look, Stephanie. Jane seems to be kind of hooked on me and I didn't want to hurt her feelings by being too demonstrative . . .'

'That's her problem,' she said, pulling me on top of her.

Stephanie's room was not even on the same floor as Jane's and the huge hotel was empty. So it was with a sense of privacy and relief that Stephanie and I made love. We were able to be as noisy as we wanted. At a crucial and somewhat audible point in our lovemaking, we both heard a rustling sound coming from the door. The small lamp on the night table was on, but the only other source of illumination was the hallway light that seeped under the gap beneath the door. It was to this horizontal strip of light that our attention was directed, for the sound was that of something being pushed under the door. The gap between the bottom of the door and the wooden floor was unusually large, maybe three inches wide. This allowed us to see the thin feminine fingers that slowly slid a letter under the door. Then the light stopped oozing in from the hallway, as a figure sat down on the floor outside Stephanie's door and just waited. I could feel the heaviness of that form – not its weight, but a sense of its being drawn down to the ground by despair and hopelessness, by a fatigue of the soul.

'My God,' whispered Stephanie. 'Who could that be?'

Of course, I knew. Certainly it could have been room service, or even a note from the concierge, but I knew from whom that message came and I knew that she was waiting outside for my answer.

I raised one finger to my lips to signal Stephanie to remain silent as I walked over to the doorway. I was naked and a little frightened. I actually had a sense of being violated, as if someone had walked uninvited into a space that should have been respected as mine. On top of that, I knew that I had forgotten to lock the door.

I reached down and picked up the sealed envelope, and returned to bed to open it. It contained a card with a picture of a landscape printed on it and a message from Jane. The letter was dated that night and the time that she had written next to the date was five minutes earlier than my watch currently read. If our watches were synchronised that would have meant she wrote the letter there in the hallway, outside Stephanie's room, amidst the sounds of lovemaking that must have been clearly and painfully audible.

This, the first of a series of letters I would receive from Jane, was a tentative, pathetic invitation to be alone with her. The commonplace nature of the words made the venue and timing of the delivery even more unnerving. Stephanie seemed visibly shaken and somewhat angry. After all, it was her room.

The next day we all met for breakfast as if nothing had happened, with the exception that Jane looked angry with me. I sat next to her and said, 'Today let's try to find time to talk.' She broke out into a broad smile and said 'Thank you', as if nothing weird had transpired the night before.

Sarah and Anna joined us and we all ordered three-minute eggs. For some reason Anna's egg was not completely cooked and she made a point of calling the waiter over. In her thick German accent she said, 'Vat do you call zis?' and tapped the offending egg with her spoon.

'It is a soft-boiled egg, a three-minute egg to be precise,' said the officious Italian waiter, as if it had implied a question of national integrity.

'Using whose clock?' questioned the digital German.

At this point I switched my egg with Anna's to bring the conversation to a halt. I had noticed a strange exchange of eye contact between Sarah and Jane and decided that Anna had said enough. Sarah excused herself and refused to speak to either Anna or me.

It was to be a long, strange day. We had only one day in Italy and only one day with the whole team. As it happened, Sarah decided that she did not need a historian or a photographer (and certainly not a photographer's assistant) on the journey to the South of France and then to Paris that we would begin that afternoon.

I was already saddened by the thought of continuing the journey without Stephanie and now I had to travel with a silent Duchess. We were to visit Villa Clara, a place that Victoria had often used as a vacation spot. It was then owned by a railway tycoon but had passed to the hands of the Branca family, the wealthy producers of Fernet-Branca liqueur. You might have seen it; it is a dark liqueur that comes in a black bottle with a vampire on the label. This fitted my mood perfectly that morning.

Before visiting the Brancas I located Jane and said, 'We'll have time to talk later about us – but what on earth is wrong with the Duchess?'

'Oh, Allan!' she exclaimed. 'Why, it's the incident with Anna. It has nothing to do with you. She loves being with you and when the three of us are together she is very happy, she is not angry with you, but the incident this morning with Anna and the egg . . .' and she rolled her eyes as if to say, 'Need I say more?'

I personally have little tolerance for restaurant complainers, those affected people who think it is a sign of good breeding and elegance to send back their food. On the other hand, Anna's comments were somewhat harmless. Nevertheless, I was not willing to share the next several days with a silent Duchess, a midnight stalker and a complaining secretary. So I confronted Sarah. 'I understand you are upset with Anna,' I began.

'JANE!' she cried out. Upon the arrival of the now terrified dresser she continued, 'Why did you tell Starkie?'

'I am sorry, ma'am, he asked me and I . . .'

'Well, Starkie,' she said, now turning towards me, 'it is nothing, it is absolutely unimportant.'

'Oh, I am glad to hear that' or 'What a relief' is what I might have said, but Sarah continued without enough of a pause for me to squeeze in any answer at all.

'But who the hell does she think she is, embarrassing me like that? Does she think she is the Queen?'

I have always believed that it is wise to choose one's battles when possible and I was not about to have one over Anna's three-minute egg, so I suggested, 'I can easily send her back to Milan with the others and we can go on without her.'

This seemed to quiet the Duchess. She was now offered the opportunity to appear gracious. 'Well,' she began magnanimously, 'let us not make too large an issue out of this. Do me a favour, Starkie – control her and see that it does not happen again, but never tell her that I was angry about it. In fact, don't ever mention it . . .'

And with that we drove through the town of Stressa to Villa Clara. As we entered the town, the Duchess saw the sign with the name of the town on it and started laughing hysterically. It actually was a frightening sound. 'That is it, that is it . . . I am in *STRESS*-a, ha, ha, ha,' she shrieked. Clearly she needed a vacation.

We met the Branca family for tea and Robin took some photos of Villa Clara for the book. We had planned on making an early start on the long drive to France, but then we were told that the Brancas had invited their entire family and friends for a reception at their Villa in honour of the visit. This was the final straw for the stressed-out Duchess. 'Get me out of here, Starkie,' she whispered in a strange, sing-song way into my ear. 'Get me out of here, find a reason, but get me out of here.' I approached the most senior of the Branca clan and apologetically pointed out that the Duchess had plans in Milan and we had only a short time to participate in the lunch party. They looked stunned but were good sports. After an hour we said our goodbyes and drove off. As I hugged Stephanie and kissed her goodbye (chastely on the cheek), she looked over at me, then at Jane, and just shook her head as if to say 'Good luck'. It was now just the four of us and we had no concrete plans. Sarah thought 'it would be fun to just drive around the South of France and soak up the atmosphere'. This meant no real agenda, no reservations and no plan – a certain recipe for disaster.

It is a very long drive from Stressa to Nice and the day got warm. I began to feel uncomfortable in my sweater and pulled the car over to get a light shirt from my bag in the boot. As I opened my door Jane's door also popped open, as if it were spring-loaded to mine. She followed me behind the car as I opened the boot. I pulled out a polo shirt and hesitated with it in my hand. She was silently inventorying me with her eyes. Finally, almost timidly, I pulled my sweater over my head and watched her eyes sink to stare hungrily at my naked chest. My skin was glistening with perspiration and she just stood there staring at it, as if she could devour me right there on the street. I quickly pulled the fresh shirt over my head, but could still feel her eyes boring through me. 'I am hot, too,' she said breathlessly, finally breaking that interminable silence. I took out an identical shirt in hunter green and handed it to her. It had my initials embroidered on it and she looked at them, and at the shirt, as if it were a holy relic. Of course, I knew I would never get it back. She put it on immediately in the back of the car and it remained a second skin for some time to come.

It was a long drive to the South of France and Sarah and I took turns driving and navigating while Jane and Anna slept in the back seat. During that long drive Sarah really opened up about her fears and feelings and began some very directed inquiries into John's financial and social status in America. I guess she could tell what I was thinking, because at one point she exclaimed (without provocation), 'You know, Starkie, I have two daughters to support.'

As it began to get dark we reached Monte Carlo. From the road we could look down at the lights and imagine the excitement that was beginning. 'Why don't we spend the first night there?' I suggested, for the bright lights of Monte Carlo are a tantalising sight after a long drive.

'That would be wonderful,' was Sarah's first response, echoed by the chorus from the back seat.

'Oh,' she then mused, 'I can't be seen in Monte Carlo . . . it is too dangerous. It's only been two months . . .'

'You're right, Your Royal Highness,' said the ever-supportive Jane. 'We dare not risk it.'

'Oh, be reasonable,' I protested. 'We can get you a dark wig or something.'

Again Sarah was sorely tempted. She needed a release and the lights down below certainly suggested that the Grand Casino of the Hôtel de Paris would be a good place to find it. After several more moments of contemplation, she said firmly, 'No – I simply must not.' So we drove on in search of a more secretive resting place.

She continued navigating but was tired and not really paying attention. Somehow she got us off the highway onto a small road that led to a fortress in the hills which Napoleon had used. We drove up a steep hill to the fortress. There was a hotel there too and I went out to see if they had rooms. It was fully booked and as I walked toward the car I realised that Jane had slipped into the passenger seat, next to Sarah, who had taken the wheel. I approached the car shaking my head to indicate that there were no rooms and was startled to see Sarah drive off. She kept the speed to a level where I could just barely keep up by running as fast as I could. Each time I got close she would speed up, to the immense pleasure of Jane who was convulsing with laughter. In all the years I knew Jane, I believe that was the only time I ever really saw her laugh. Finally at the bottom of the hill she stopped and let me into the back of the car.

'Nice stroll, Starkie?' she asked.

'You seem to be perspiring,' added Jane.

While reading Victoria's diaries early the next morning, Sarah was to discover that Victoria's carriage had taken the same false route and also ended at the foot of the same fortification, although history has never documented whether Victoria drove off leaving Albert to run after her. It was such coincidences that began to convince the Duchess (and consequently Jane) that she was the incarnation of Victoria, retracing her own steps. To quote her final draft of the book's foreword:

> Outside Nice I was seized with a sudden, very strong impulse to turn off the motorway and take the winding, mountainous road through La Turbie and Eze, going far out of my way through magical places, only to find later, without realising it, I had been following the route the Queen took. With hindsight, 'wrong turnings' seemed to become a pattern, and I felt more certain that we were meant to visit these places.

I had been very nervous about the issue of not having hotel reservations for the night. Sarah felt the need for a journey without constraints and, as she wrote in her diary of 7 November, 'I had insisted on no prior bookings so that I could keep my spontaneity.' There are many places in the world where one can enjoy the charm of an unplanned vacation; there is something adventurous and spontaneous about stopping at the hotel that appeals to you on the spur of the moment. Let me say that the South of France is not a place suited for such spontaneity. Each hotel claimed to be fully booked and none believed me when I explained the identity of my companion who waited in the car. As the hours passed we began to wonder if we would be able to find anywhere that would take us in. Finally, Sarah decided that she would personally ask for a room at the next hotel. The Belle Aire Hôtel in Cap Ferrat is one of the most exclusive resorts in that rather exclusive region and when we stopped at its front door I pointed out, 'Remember, we have a budget . . .'

'Don't worry, I will ask for the cheapest rooms they have,' replied the determined Duchess as she exited the car alone. 'Stay here, Jane,' she ordered. This was 1992 – Sarah had been *the* international headline grabber for the last ten weeks. Can you imagine the look on the receptionist's face when she entered that hotel, unescorted and without a reservation, to ask for four rooms? I can answer that (although I had not accompanied her inside), for when she came out to get us the entire staff of the hotel was following like rats behind the Pied Piper, all with the same hypnotised look on their faces.

'You did it!' I exclaimed.

'Of course, Starkie,' she replied with pride. 'Bad news, though. They insisted on giving me the royal suite. Better call JB.' Jane was to share the luxury of the royal suite with her mistress and Anna and I were given rooms on another floor.

We agreed to dress for dinner and meet at the bar at nine. This would have given me the chance to take a nap for about an hour, but as I entered my room the phone was already ringing. It was Jane.

'Can I see you now?' she asked. 'I really need to see you alone . . . and you promised.'

I looked longingly at my bed, but realised that I needed to clear the air with Jane before we began this period of planned relaxation in the South of France.

'Can I have 15 minutes to shower and change?' I asked with resignation.

'Of course,' she purred. 'I will see you at the bar.'

I arrived first and ordered a drink. I was a little behind in my diaries and grabbed the bar napkin and started writing the events of the last two days on it when I was interrupted by the adjacent bar stool being moved. I looked up and saw a very attractive, glamorous and sexy lady whose physiognomy resembled that of Jane Dunn-Butler – but that is where the similarities ended. This willowy young blonde was wearing a tight dark skirt with a slit up the side and very high heels that set off the shape of her legs. Her white blouse was loose and tucked in at the midriff, accentuating the narrowness of her waist as well as the length of her legs. Her hair, finally freed from that ever-present hair band, cascaded in a wave along the side of her face, bouncing softly as she took her seat. She had applied a fair amount of eye make-up and a glistening sort of lipstick that made one concentrate on her mouth and eyes and somehow disregard the incongruities of her bone structure. This was a pretty girl and, what is more, this girl looked and *acted* sexy.

'Were you waiting long?' she asked with a smile. Before I could answer she continued, 'I needed to draw the bath for Her Royal Highness and lay out her clothes.' Of course, I already knew that it was Jane, but that statement was the first jolt of reality that reminded me that it was the *same* Jane! Her whole appearance, conduct, and manner, or as psychologists love to call the sum of all the parts of a person, her *Gestalt*, was totally different – startlingly different. Even more disconcerting was the fact that she *knew* it.

'What are you writing?' she asked, looking down at the napkin.

'I am just catching up on my diary of our trips.'

'Am I in it?' she teased.

'Well, that depends . . .' I said, realising as I said it that I was taking the bait and flirting right back. I caught myself and decided that I had better steer this into safer ground, so I began again with the question, 'What did you want to talk to me about?'

'Well, first I wanted to give you something,' she said quietly. It was then that I realised she held a small package in her hand.

'Please,' she said, handing it to me.

I was surprised and embarrassed. After the bizarre episode of the previous night, the last thing I expected was a gift. I believe she guessed what I was thinking, for she simply said, 'I wanted to give it to you last night, but . . .'

Realising that it would be ungracious to accept a gift while admonishing her for her behaviour, I said nothing and unwrapped the small package. Inside was an old book, bound in green leather, with faded golden letters that read '*Wuthering Heights* by E. Brontë', dated 1883. It was a valuable second edition of our favourite masterpiece. I was speechless, touched and even a little ashamed.

'I can't accept this, Jane,' I said.

'You must,' she insisted. 'I am sorry it is not a first edition, but it was the best that I could afford.'

I did not know how to react. On one level I was noticing her as a woman for the first time, while on the other hand her last sentence reminded me of her vulnerability. Still, I was deeply moved and grateful.

Inside the book was a small envelope with a letter telling me that I was her Heathcliff and that she could give me the love I deserved. 'I didn't want to damage the book by writing in it directly,' she explained. Of course, that reminded me how she must have valued that purchase. I thought of the things she would not be able to buy for herself on account of this extravagance. It also struck me as odd that Jane felt that her personalisation of the book would diminish its value. Of course I was not interested in its resale value, so her pathetic concern that her inscription would have been unwelcome was very sad indeed.

'Jane, I am really touched, but this is too valuable a gift. I don't even know how you could have found it.'

'I got it in London,' she went on, 'and I really want you to *have* it.' She delivered that last line with a look of pure desire, so I was fairly certain that the 'it' was not just the book. As she spoke, her legs wrapped around the back of mine and she actually drew our stools together, sliding them over the green marble floor of the bar. As our knees touched, I embraced her. Her arms wrapped around my back and her legs encircled mine – and I realised that I was enjoying it. She kissed with something more than passion, with a sense of desperation, a hunger, giving me a feeling that she was sucking something out of me, or perhaps trying desperately to link herself to me. Her hands did not move along my back, but clung to me with the desperation of a person trying to freeze time. The intensity was frightening and intriguing and, I must admit, arousing. Maybe John and Sarah were right, I thought. She seemed to again read my mind. 'You chose the wrong girl, Allan,' she began. 'Maybe you have always chosen the wrong ones. I could give you *so* much more.' With that we were kissing again and I was getting more excited. I am sure that one might think I just got carried away with the moment and the sense of

---

* Scotland Yard was very interested in ascertaining where Jane had purchased the book. The prosecution had some evidence which indicated that Jane might have been less than truthful and there might be a possibility that the book came from the royal archives.

gratitude for her generosity and thoughtfulness. But that was not exactly it. This was a very sexy woman, another Jane, who looked and acted totally differently from the Jane I had known before. This was not the docile servant who seemed to live for her mistress's slightest whim, nor was she the poor victim who was secretly mourning the absence of unqualified love. This was an overtly sexual creature who was able to readily stimulate arousal and lust.

Now, let me point out that I was not sleeping with my own secretary, but when Anna Delnef appeared during the finale of this scene I was as embarrassed as if my wife had caught me in flagrante delicto. I had complained to Anna about Jane's overwhelming interest in me and had even told her about the note under Stephanie's door. I realised that I must now seem like a total fool, and I knew it was pointless to explain that this was a *different* Jane. So I said the only thing I could think of: 'What would you like to drink, Anna?' Realising that I had not even had time to order Jane a drink, I decided to ask her too. As I ordered the drinks Anna smiled at me and said, 'Vom kleinen Kopf gesteuert'. It is a colourful German expression, which translated literally means 'steered by one's little head'.

It took another ten minutes for Sarah to join us and by then the three of us had become a little tipsy. It had been many hours since we had eaten a hurried meal at the Brancas', and even longer since the 'incident' with the three-minute egg. Sarah was stone-cold sober and her delay had been caused by a conversation with John which had made her remember how much she missed him. The evening had all the ingredients of a Noel Coward play. We had a tired Duchess steeped in Victorian romance, longing for her reunion with John, a love-starved Jane now smelling blood (mine) and wanting more and my embarrassed secretary, who was still socially exiled as a result of the breakfast fiasco.

As I sat across from the Duchess with Jane on one side and Anna on the other I felt a premonition of disaster. The Duchess began by saying that John was well and missed both of us. 'Well, I will call him tonight. I miss him too,' I answered and really meant it. The press has vilified John but that does not change the fact that he is enormous fun and was truly my best friend. 'He told me not to worry about the cost of the suite,' she went on. 'He said, "I will buy you the hotel".'

That would be quite a trick, I thought. He had just spent every penny he had on the trips they had already taken together and had borrowed money from his father to pay the legal costs associated with trying to stop publication of the South of France photos. John's total assets at this time consisted of his illiquid shares of our troubled construction company, a squash racket and five Savile Row suits.

As if Sarah had somehow thought of John's wardrobe at the same time, she continued by asking, 'So, Starkie, what do you think of those cream shirts that I got for JB?'

'Very big change,' I replied, avoiding my first impulse to say that I hated them.

'Did you notice all the nice bits?' she went on, smiling at Jane and adding, 'Jane had them made up for me on Jermyn Street.' John had shown me, in gory detail, all 'the nice bits', which included: collar stays in sterling with secret messages engraved in Sarah's own handwriting; a special oversized pocket for John's mobile phone, with which the lovers were able to remain in almost constant communication; and even secret embroidered messages on the cuffs, with their code names for one another. I thought how I missed his old white shirts.

'Did you see how I have him do his hair now?' she continued. This might seem odd, since everyone knows that John is bald. Well, what Sarah had done was to convince John that he should grease down the hair on the side and back of his head with a special hair oil which Sarah had discovered. It resembled saddle soap and John would scoop out a palmful and slick down his hair with it. It made him perspire profusely and it seemed that the beads of sweat which emerged were constituted from wax, not salt water. But this was only step one. Later, Sarah convinced John to use a strange hair restorative which had apparently been recommended by a member of her family. It made John's scalp flake and peel like a leper, a process Sarah called 'snowing', and pronounced that it was the first step towards 'new hair'. Judging by recent photos, I assume that John is still awaiting the 'new hair'.

'And the ties, Starkie – what about the ties?' she crooned. Here Jane was the real culprit. It was Jane who did the clothes shopping and those strange Hermès ties (of which I had already been a reluctant recipient) contained patterns of such distracting imagination that business meetings were often interrupted by debates about their meaning.

I think it is odd that Sarah had such confidence in Jane's taste in clothes. She would be sent out on shopping expeditions with a virtual carte blanche. I agree that some of her choices were very good, for instance the Ralph Lauren outfits she chose for Sarah were very becoming. The problem seemed to arise when Jane chose clothing that did not fit her limited social and business experience. Thus, the formal wear that she selected for Sarah was often harshly criticised and the neckties that she chose for us should have been.

'S-T-A-R-K-I-E . . .' she drawled, as if the best were yet to come and the anticipation to be savoured, and now she tapped two fingers against her wrist. 'The cufflinks?'

Here I had to agree. Sarah had a great imagination with designing jewellery, and her creation of imaginative cufflinks was impressive. Jane had assisted with some of these creations and would one day even work for the jeweller who turned these ideas into bejewelled reality. The assortment of cufflinks for John's new shirt collection included miniature Budgies, nicknames in code and the pièce de résistance: cherry trees. In their complex code of love, cherry trees was the couple's way of saying 'I love you', in places where inquisitive ears would be attuned to every word. Sarah had had a set of golden cufflinks fashioned to look like cherry trees, with rubies as the cherries. They were beautiful. John managed to lose them a number of times, often leaving them in the rooms of other women, but it would not be until a year after his relationship with Sarah ended that he would lose them for good.

I do not mean to sound cynical about Sarah's gifts. She was a great gift-giver. I do not mean to sound too judgmental about Jane's taste in implementing her mistress's ideas either. Both meant well. The thing that bothered me on this particular evening was that Sarah was trying to imply that she was improving John, trying to change him. This bothered me for two reasons. First, I think that it is dangerous to try to change your partner during a relationship and, second, we had just spent the last two trips preaching back and forth to each other how wonderful Victoria's unqualified acceptance of Albert had been. I am not suggesting that changing the colour of a fellow's shirt is a major request. What I understood Sarah to be saying was that she was improving John in many ways and so I confronted her on the issue.

'Well, yes, Starkie, you are right. He does need to change more than his wardrobe, he needs to be more humble, to listen more,' and she went on to explain how she intended to enact these modifications.

'Do you really think you will change him?' I asked. 'You will only start a chain reaction of resentment that will undermine the relationship. Can't you just accept him and love him the way he is?' I looked over at Jane for support and she averted her eyes. 'Come on, Jane!' I urged. 'I thought you were the great one for unqualified love.'

This was unfair and I regret it still. I had no right to pit Jane against her employer. She tried to find a diplomatic way around it.

'I do agree, Allan, but I also see that Her Royal Highness does have unqualified love – she is just trying to help him improve.'

'That's it, Jane,' said Sarah. 'You see, Starkie, in a relationship both partners are like two trees growing intertwined towards the sun.'

I should have conceded there but I did not. I suppose I was still upset at the questions she had asked on the drive to France. Assuming she was interested in John's pretended wealth, her insistence on changing him seemed like more evidence that she was not really in love with him. I lashed out in a harsh monologue about acceptance which had her crying within minutes. Jane looked upset with me and even Anna whispered to me in German that I was attacking her due to other issues and I ought to stop. We finished our dinner quietly and Sarah went up to bed, saying 'Goodnight, we had better get some rest, we will see you at breakfast', and with a jerk of her head motioned Jane to follow her. Jane looked over her shoulder at me as she walked behind her angry mistress, simultaneously raising her eyebrows in a look of uncertainty and shrugging her shoulders in resignation. She was sharing a suite with Sarah and the message was 'I don't think I can come to you.' The Duchess was, after all, not Her Majesty and therefore not in the habit of using the royal 'we'; the plural in this case meant that two people needed rest.

Anna remained with me to discuss what had happened. We were both surprised at my own anger towards Sarah and my new interest in Jane. I went to my room and waited up for a few minutes, but there were no calls and no midnight notes under my door. Jane was consoling her angry mistress and it was to get worse the next day.

CHAPTER SIX

THE HEADACHE

THE NEXT MORNING was warm and sunny. It was November, but mild enough to feel like a day in June. The hotel was on a hill that rolled gently down to the sea and the Duchess decided to have breakfast on the patio. I arrived after she and Jane had already begun and felt an immediate chill the moment they saw me. They sat side by side, both wearing dark sunglasses, whispering to one another. I felt as though I were intruding, and asked permission to join them. 'Good morning,' I said, trying to break the ice. Two heads bobbed in silent synchronised response. Four eyes peered at me, safe behind dark glass. I ordered breakfast and gave up my initial attempts at conversation, seeing that it was futile. A waiter came to pour my coffee and the two heads turned in unison to follow his movements.

'Lovely,' said one head.

'Delicious,' said the other.

'I noticed him earlier,' continued the first. And together they turned to watch him withdraw.

'I think I will walk down to the beach,' I said, feeling slightly ill at ease.

'Are you already packed?' asked the Duchess.

'I thought we were staying here for a couple of days,' I responded with surprise.

'No. We need to check out in less than an hour to get the 10.08 Paris train from Nice.'

This was a surprise. There were a number of places in the area Sarah had planned to visit for her research and, on top of that, the

Jane's 'Wuthering Heights'. She would forever be haunted by the
deadly passions of Brontë's tortured characters, October 1992.

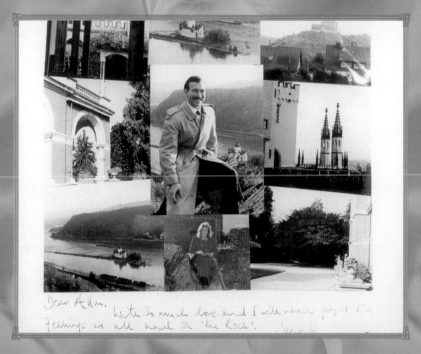

Dear Allan,
With so much love and I will never forget the
feelings we all had on 'the Rock'. Sarah

In this photo collage the Duchess of York commemorated the strong emotions she shared with Jane
and the author on the windswept German hilltop Jane had dubbed 'Wuthering Heights'.

Presented by the Duchess of York to the author at the end of a whirlwind week in NY prior to jetting back to London on Concorde with Jane, February 1994.

To My Best Friend Stankie, I miss you so much, I miss your laughter, honesty, total pure kind heart - I love my brother/Best friend relationship - and really really cherish and treasure it - thank you my friend.
Sarah. 16.2.94.
(whoops in early for Sarah)

Throughout her nine years with the Duchess of York, Jane's main rival was Sarah's PA Jane Ambler, pictured here with a witch's hat during a fancy-dress party at Romenda Lodge.

Jane's four-year-long seduction of the author would finally be consummated shortly after this last innocent embrace, June 1995, Krakow, Poland.

Fergie and Jane held court in a villa in the South of France while John Bryan (standing), the author and friends enjoyed a hedonistic jet-set lifestyle in Sardinia, summer of 1994.

This photo of Princesses Beatrice and Eugenie was used for a joint Christmas card sent to the author by the Duke and Duchess of York, 1993.

Leaving Jane behind, the Duchess of York and the author taking an equestrian break in Ireland, spring of 1994.

Another of Sarah's beloved photo collages — this time commemorating a
successful charity excursion to Albania, 1993.

FRIDAY 6TH NOV
12:05 am

Dear Allan,
        I've been trying
to find the right words
all evening to say how
much I have missed
you since arriving back
from Germany, and I didn't

want to wait until tomorrow
to say this. please believe
what I am saying, I really
wanted to say this to you
to your face, tonight but
well...
        I really would like more
time to talk with you.

Jane x

During Jane's obsession with seducing the author she pushed this pathetic note under the door of
the hotel room of another woman in which the author was making love, then waited for a
response. Scotland Yard used the note as evidence. Note the startling similarity in
Jane's handwriting to that of the Duchess.

John Bryan (right), the author and their respective private secretaries outside
their corporate headquarters in Frankfurt, 1995.

Thomas Cressman and Jane in happier times.

By 1997 'Lady Jane's' metamorphosis was complete. At this point Sarah and Jane's appearances were so similar that even the press confused them. © Alpha

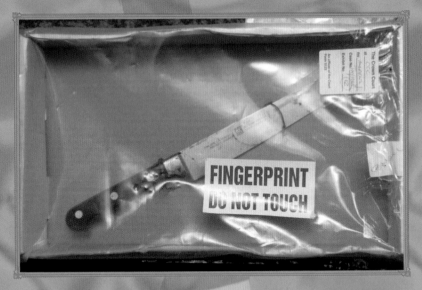

The eight-inch razor-sharp German kitchen knife that Jane thrust into Thomas's chest. © PA

Dangling from the bannister one can see the blood-stained cord of Jane's dressing-gown, which she used to tie the bedroom door closed after her brutal attack on Thomas. © PA

rental car had to be disposed of and preparations made for Paris. Sarah, noting my concern and perhaps recognising that her punishment was somewhat harsh, said, 'Oh Starkie, we can stay for a couple of days in Paris and go dancing and have a real laugh, and we need to visit Versailles anyway for the book.' With that she arose and returned to her suite. I looked at Jane incredulously. 'Is she that angry still?' I asked.

'You were rather hard on her last night,' replied the old familiar Jane, the one with the hair band and averted eyes.

'Of all people, I thought you would agree,' I responded.

'Well, yes, I do, I completely agree with you about unqualified and unconditional love, but she is very upset right now.'

It seemed that the illusive love both ladies sought was ideal in a theoretical sense, but that as part of a real relationship it was too restrictive. The woman sitting next to me had as little in common with the willowy blonde of the night before as Sarah had with Queen Victoria's ideals of love. I looked at Jane, shielded still behind her mistress's glasses, with a feeling of pity and revulsion.

'She didn't seem upset with you, Jane,' I pointed out.

'Oh Allan, that is because the most wonderful thing has happened and Her Royal Highness was telling me all about it.'

'Has John agreed to listen more and become more humble?' I asked with sarcasm.

Jane rolled her eyes, then said, 'The Duchess was reading Queen Victoria's diary this morning and in it Victoria had written that she made the same wrong turn as we did last night! Imagine that – couldn't you tell that she was in the car with us last night?'

'It was a simple navigation mistake,' I answered impatiently.

'There is more – as we were sitting here before you arrived, the Duchess pointed out that the trees looked like umbrellas.'

This was far from a revelation. Along the coast of the South of France, the foliage of the pine trees often grows in a canopy, in an opposite direction to the wind from the ocean. Such trees bordered the patio where we now sat.

'And, Allan . . .' she gasped, 'just before you arrived, while she was eating her croissant, she glanced at Victoria's diary about this region and it described the trees as "umbrellas".'

'Well, that is just a small coincidence.'

'Oh, don't be so negative. Victoria is with us and the Duchess is certain that she has been here in this very hotel and is with us now. I am going to check with the manager and see if they have a record of her visit.'

There was only time for a quick walk to the beach. I thought of how nice the next two days could have been had I remained silent the night before.

Bernard, the hotel manager, informed a disappointed Jane that there was no evidence that Victoria had ever been in residence, but by way of consolation he was kind enough to drive us to Nice and return our rented car. Ease of travel was one of the most valuable things Sarah would leave behind were she really to divorce Andrew. There is first-class travel, then VIP travel and then the rarified world of royal travel, where tickets, departure times, customs and bureaucrats have no power. It is a beautiful place.

As we were checking out of the hotel, Jane urged me to apologise. I was accustomed to paying for our accommodation jointly on my card, but this time Sarah refused and paid her own way. I looked at this as an even more formidable form of rejection and took Jane's advice. 'Ma'am, I am very sorry for what I said last night,' I began.

'Nonsense, Starkie, I like a good argument sometimes,' was her gracious response.

As we waited on the platform for the Paris train I stood next to Sarah, who remained silent, and noticed that tears were running down her face beneath her dark glasses. Jane motioned to me to step a few feet away and then said in a strangely pained voice, 'She has a terrible migraine, she didn't really sleep last night.'

'Did I cause it?' I asked with a mixture of scepticism and guilt.

'No, I don't think so, she just gets them sometimes when she is under a lot of pressure.'

Jane promptly returned to the side of her mistress and I looked at their faces, or at least what was visible, and noticed that the muscles around their temples were pinched in exactly the same expression of agony. It was reminiscent of those famous religious martyrs who, through intense prayer, could physically induce the stigmata – the holy wounds of Christ. Had Jane been born in another century she might either have been canonised or burned.

After a short wait in the station, we loaded the endless pieces of luggage into the train and entered the vacant first-class compartment. I instinctively slid next to Sarah, but she turned on me

as if I had the plague and screamed, 'I need space
I moved to the seat ahead of her and talked quietl
enough. Sarah burst into tears and fled to
compartment, where she sat alone and wept. Finall
diary and her large red Mont Blanc fountain pei
quite a production – and began writing feverishly
describe her feelings on the train.

> Tears rolled down my face and thankfully my sunglasses were
> close at hand. I longed to be in a blackened room, with fresh
> air cascading through my veins. I really need to be free now.
> This terrible strain of uncertainty cannot go on any longer.

'Her Royal Highness needs to be alone,' announced Jane in the tones
of a lady-in-waiting.

'Wow, that is a surprise,' I responded with annoyance. After all,
Sarah had just made that rather clear.

Anna and Jane began to talk and so I decided to move to another
seat as well. Sarah was still writing and looking over Victoria's
diaries, as if she might find some answers to her own troubles in
them. She was supposed to be viewing the countryside to comment
on its changes since Victoria made this train trip, and so she would
occasionally peer out of the window and then write a few more lines.
Jane had been watching her as closely as I had and at a particular
point decided that it was safe to join her mistress. She took leave of
Anna and actually curtseyed to the sitting Duchess, asking
permission to be seated. She looked like a beaten dog which
approaches its angry master, tail stuck firmly between its legs, then
shamelessly licks the hand that struck it. Jane seemed most obsessed
by excruciatingly precise protocol when the Duchess was at her
worst. Somehow it seemed to work for her. In a few minutes, the two
were chatting happily and even giggling. The emotional weather was
prone to change so rapidly in those early days. What they were
hatching, as I was soon to learn, was a plan to allow Jane to continue
developing the success she had begun to achieve with me the night
before. Sadly, the willowy blonde of the previous evening had
diminished into an obsequious sycophant.

Suddenly Sarah and Jane emerged from behind dark glasses and
feigned migraines and, with broad smiles, announced, 'We are

hungry!' What transpired next was astounding. The first-class cabin was not connected directly to the restaurant car and one had to leave the train, then re-enter it several compartments further down. I timed the stops – we had less than 90 seconds to make the switch and over 20 pieces of luggage to carry with us.

'Come on, Starkie,' teased the Duchess, 'aren't you up for it?'

'You are so strong, Allan,' added the pliant Jane (when in her obsequious mode, Jane was often overly complimentary at random). 'I am sure you can carry most of the bags.'

Coaxed by the Duchess and her shadow, the group managed to relocate to the back of the train where we were rewarded with stale ham sandwiches and soda. That was fine. Sarah had recovered, and now taunting me and eating bad food were amusing her. Jane felt instrumental in the recovery and was newly bonded with her mistress, so she too shone with self-satisfaction and good cheer. 'Anna,' cried the Duchess, 'let us go and have some tea together,' and with that the two ladies left Jane and me alone in the compartment. As time crept by, I could see Sarah and Anna taking turns peeking through the glass window of the adjacent compartment to see how we were faring.

Once alone, Jane began the assault with renewed zeal. My behaviour of the night before had obviously given her reason to hope and the significance of the subsequent events had not registered. To Jane, we were about to continue where we had left off at the bar last night. She placed her hand on my leg and looked at me with very apparent affection.

'I really enjoyed our talk last night,' she began, and her hand moved a little higher up my leg.

'Well, I am sorry for the way things turned out,' I responded.

'Oh, we will have other times,' she said confidently.

'Jane – you are a married woman and I am sorry that things went a little too far.'

'That doesn't matter,' she responded. 'I don't really have strong feelings for him, I feel sorry for him, really; IBM is about to make him redundant or something. He is just not ambitious and he is a lot older than me.'

I had not yet met Christopher at this time, but in truth he was 20 years her senior and a nice but unattractive fellow. I do not simply mean that he was physically plain; he had very little charisma and seemed to lack drive. I can imagine why they married. She was initially proud of his family, he possessed a double-barrelled last name and his father had been an officer. Jane was a servant living in the servants' quarters of Buckingham Palace when she met him. The large emerald engagement ring that he had given her created a stir among the other servants in the palace. She might have been working for a royal duchess but she was still very much the humble servant from Grimsby. When they married in August 1990 she regarded the alliance as socially desirable. One has only to look at her wedding pictures to see that. She married Christopher in the Church of the Holy Trinity and St Mary in Grimsby. Both Jane's mother and grandmother had been married there and, in relation to their humble lives, Jane was a returning heroine. The wedding was rather theatrical, with the Grimsby Orpheus Male Voice Choir performing during the ceremony. Jane wore a very Victorian-looking wedding dress made of raw silk, with a wreath of silk flowers forming the somewhat plunging neckline and her head was crowned with a tiara. Even then poor Jane had illusions of grandeur, but in the case of Christopher those illusions were soon outgrown, then revised. I was to be the idealisation of the first revision. If you follow Jane's three obsessions you will note a degree of similarity in the outward appearance and trappings of success of Thomas Cressman, Dimitri Horne and me.

Deciding to take another tack I pointed out once again, 'I have a girlfriend.'

'Yes, Her Royal Highness told me.'

'I told you!' I reminded her.

'What I meant to say,' she replied with waning patience, 'is that Her Royal Highness told me that John does not like her.'

'He doesn't have to!' I exclaimed.

'Allan,' she began as if speaking to an idiot child, 'the Duchess, John and I are your friends and we understand what is best for you. You have a tendency to choose the wrong people – people that use you because you are afraid to be happy.'

This was too much. Jane, a woman barely in possession of her own personality, was trying to analyse mine.

'Just give me a chance,' she continued.

Taking yet another tack, I offered: 'I like you, Jane, but the timing is wrong.'

'Why?' she demanded harshly.

'Because there are other people involved.'

'So,' she queried, 'if there were no other people involved would you give me a try?'

This seemed like a safe way out, so I took the bait. 'Probably, but that is academic at this point.'

'I don't think so,' she continued, expanding on the beachhead she had achieved. 'We can see how we get on and then decide about the other people. You already are doing that with Stephanie and you have a girlfriend at home, so . . .'

I must admit that she had me there so, trying to wiggle out of this trap, I explained, 'At the moment I am trying to decide between my current girlfriend and Stephanie. It would be too disruptive and unfair to begin a relationship with you until I know where I stand.'

'They are both wrong for you!' she exclaimed. 'I keep telling you that they are the same type of person – I could make you so much more happy.'

For over two hours this conversation continued. Jane was insistent, sure of herself, and used good logic. It was an awkward and frustrating conversation because Jane was simply not willing to concede, and I was absolutely committed to not encouraging her again. The brief moment of sexual attraction that I had experienced the night before had evaporated completely and I was confronted with an insistent woman unwilling to take no for an answer. By this time I had begun to regard Jane as a close friend and I would continue to do so for many years. As a result I was trying not to hurt her feelings; yet anything I seemed to say out of politeness was taken as weakness or capitulation, and would be followed by renewed enthusiasm.

Looking back on my early conversations with Jane, I can understand the frustration Thomas Cressman must have felt in dealing with her. I learned from the descriptions provided by his surviving friends that Tommy was kind-hearted and not overly assertive with Jane. Having experienced Jane's unwavering insistence, I can see how Tommy might have been coerced through affection and guilt to maintain a relationship with her, despite not being fully committed to marrying her. It was not easy to say no to Jane Dunn-Butler.

I was exhausted by the time that Sarah and Anna finally returned.

They must have consumed two gallons of tea as they waited for the resolution of this conversation.

'Sit near me, Starkie,' ordered the curious Duchess. 'How did it go?' she asked right off.

'Fine,' I replied with a feeling that I would have to say a lot more.

'So, is Jane your new girlfriend?'

'We sort of left it open. I mean I said that we would continue to develop our friendship but that we would wait on any romantic developments until I had more clarity.'

'Hmm. Doesn't sound like you resolved very much, does it? Well, an extraordinary thing happened to me with Anna.'

'Did you tell her about her egg?' I asked.

'No, and you'd better never tell her about it either. Listen, Starkie, you will never believe this, but Anna confessed that she was in love with me.'

'Sounds like you got further along with your conversation than Jane did,' I retorted.

'She was serious.'

'Do you want me to break the news to John?' I continued jokingly.

Now, let me step back and put this in context. Most people will only experience Sarah as an image on their televisions or a photo in the newspaper. What is not easily captured by a lens is her incredible sexuality. Through her gestures, eye contact and a certain quality that I cannot even begin to define, Sarah exudes a highly provocative sexuality which is androgynous, seeming to attract men and women indiscriminately. We would spend a lot of time over the next few years trying to figure it out and keep a head count of the victims. But I would point out to her often that the majority of her staff (both male and female) were captivated by her. She had to agree in many cases. Shortly after this episode, one of Sarah's secretaries placed a stack of papers on the floor and waited for the Duchess to enter the room. The young lady was sitting with her legs extended to either side of the papers and made no attempt to stand and curtsey. When Sarah sat down to read the material she noticed that she was forced to stare at and almost touch the intersection point of the outstretched legs (which apparently was not concealed with undergarments) in order to pick up the papers.

Another of the female assistants who was vying for Sarah's affections was so devoted and so blatantly attracted to her mistress that it became an inside joke among her inner group. Princess Esmeralda of Belgium was a mutual friend of ours and at one point I noticed that she was regarding the behaviour of this particular servant with some amusement. 'Did you ever read *Rebecca*?' I asked innocuously, and Esmeralda burst into laughter and cried out 'Mrs Danvers!' That was to become our nickname for this infatuated lady, for Mrs Danvers was the obsessively loyal lesbian servant of Mrs Rebecca De Winter.

The most extreme example of this androgynous effect would come several years later with a direct proposition from two gorgeous blondes, but for now Sarah was trying to deal with Anna's confession of love.

With such pleasant thoughts and discussions to keep us busy, we soon approached the station in Paris. As we neared the French capital Sarah's mind began to wander to John Bryan's trousers. 'He sometimes wears a pair of tight black jeans which I had Jane buy for him,' she began out of nowhere. 'He looks so good in them,' she continued, lost in a daydream. Jane had joined us by this time and nodded slowly, as if she too had followed Sarah into this vision.

'We had better decide where we are going to stay,' I said, trying to snap them out of it.

'Everyone knows what Versailles looks like! Let's go back to England – *now*!'

We will never know the magnitude of the loss to Victorian scholarship that those black jeans had precipitated, for the instant the train stopped we were off to Charles de Gaulle airport: Sarah and a lovesick Jane bound for London, Allan and a lovesick Anna bound for Frankfurt. We exchanged our now routine hugs with hurried words of eternal devotion and then said goodbye until the next trip, which was scheduled for ten days hence. Jane kissed me goodbye and with the surprising words, 'I feel so much better now that we have straightened things out,' hugged me feverishly.

All in all, it had been a long two days.

Soon after my return, I received a package couriered from England to my home in Germany. The last time that had happened the box had contained a supply of conkers, sent by a playful Sarah. This time the contents were rather different. Inside a huge Harrods box was a stuffed animal, a little dog. Around his neck he wore a tag introducing himself and saying what he liked to eat. I had seen a virtual menagerie of these animals with similar tags in John's flat. It was one of Sarah's hallmark gifts. The box was filled with dog toys and even dog biscuits. It came with a romantic card that contained the type of message Sarah would often write to Otto (JB). But this time it was written to me and this time it was from Jane. I had heard of copycat killers, but copycat gift-givers was a new twist. Thank heavens Sarah never tried her hand at serial killing!

CHAPTER SEVEN

THE REJECTION

LOOKING BACK ON the complex interaction among the three of us, it seems that the relationship between Sarah and Jane, as well as that between Jane and me, divides itself into three broad phases: the seduction, the rejection and the resurrection. The seduction was the period in which Sarah relied on Jane as her main travel companion and confidante. It began on that October day in 1992 when Sarah ventured out of exile on her first post-South of France excursions. This was the first time Jane had been singled out as more than a servant and she was offered the opportunity to be seduced by the full impact of Sarah's charm and manner. It was also the first chance for Jane to study her mistress in depth and begin the process of her metamorphosis.

The seduction period was also the time in which Jane tried her best to seduce me. It's hard to know what the true source of attraction to me might have been, but I would suggest that a component of it was the fact that I was the partner and best friend of her mistress's lover. In a sense, had Jane succeeded in her seduction and in establishing a romance with John Bryan's best friend, she would have elevated herself significantly in her relationship with Sarah.

The seduction period was one of vast change in Jane's personality. During that time she seemed to be developing two clear personae; that of the loyal, supportive servant as well as that of the seductive, charming, ostensibly self-confident (yet secretly self-hating) copy of her mistress. With each trip and each visit to Romenda Lodge, I witnessed that empty vessel, devoid of any real personality, gradually fill with the siphoned essence of her mistress's charm. Jane's manner became more aggressive and she became more unabashed in expressing her will.

This period was about to come to an end. The initial phase had started with Sarah's first outing for the Queen Victoria project and its end was heralded with her last. In the case of Sarah's relationship with Jane, the factors that began the period of the rejection were threefold. As I pointed out at the beginning of the story, Sarah had troubled relations with her servants in general. She expected too much from them and confused them with vacillating treatment, confiding far too much when she treated them as friends and compensating far too angrily when she remembered they were servants. In a sense, her staff was suffering from social whiplash. When Sarah sensed she had gone too far in her tendencies towards over-familiarity, she would compensate by reverting back to strict protocol and essentially silence the confused servant. I watched her do this countless times with myriad people, and Jane was the first and most severe example.

The alienation of one over-personalised servant relationship was inevitably followed by the creation of a second confidante. As a result, there was the constant din of in-fighting among her ranks of employees, often making me think of what must take place behind the eunuch-guarded gates of a sheik's harem. Sarah had gone too far with Jane and she began to withdraw, with her usual accompaniment of complaints. A search began for a new champion and I was called in to assist. I found Sarah a Texan lawyer whom we put on my pay roll and essentially gave to the Duchess. Next, I sent her an attractive secretary named Lisa Lewis, whom I had briefly dated, and she was hired immediately. Finally, Sarah asked me to interview her old assistant, Christine Gallagher, who had just returned from an extended stay in South Africa and was destined to return to the staff of the Duchess. At the same time the dormant Jane Ambler (former court champion) began to be reinstated in the Duchess's world.

As the Victoria trips were drawing to a close, Sarah sought another reason to continue those periods of escape which brought her a form of solace and decided to found a children's charity with a wonderful lady named Theo Ellert. The plan was that Children in

Crisis would allow Sarah the opportunity to travel throughout Eastern Europe in the hope of assisting under-privileged children.

The combination of new individuals, as well as Sarah's withdrawal from a relationship that had become too personal, resulted in Jane's excommunication from the Duchess's circle of confidant(e)s for a period of nine months. During this time I, too, tried to avoid intimate contact with Jane. As you will soon see, the rejected Jane displayed some strange and sinister characteristics which in retrospect might have served as a warning.

During the rejection it seemed as if Jane became more shrill, more demanding of attention and more frantic. But as strange as her behaviour might then have appeared, the real horror would begin during the final stage. For in those nine months of rejection, Jane seemed to have burrowed into a cocoon in which her metamorphosis continued by itself. It was a sealed period of gestation in which the embryonic creature within her was nurtured with bitterness and fear. When she emerged from this embittered period, in the final stage of the resurrection, she would explode out of her seclusion with all the force of a jack-in-the-box from hell. It would be the metamorphosed Lady Jane that would win the fight for dominance in that torn and confused shell that once housed the empty but ambitious soul of Jane Dunn-Butler.

Jane's transition from the seduction to the rejection period had already begun by the time Sarah was ready for our final research trip. We visited Berlin and Potsdam, and Sarah came alone. When I questioned her about this, she answered by shaking her head, then said, 'I just needed to leave her home this time, Starkie.'

'She told me she was coming,' I answered with some confusion.

'I just couldn't take her this time,' responded the impatient Duchess. 'She can be a little annoying,' she added.

Actually, the group seemed to miss the presence of Jane. In those days Jane tried so hard to please that people generally liked her. Stephanie, however, was grateful for her absence and admitted that she was able to enjoy my company more without the fear of hurting Jane, with less of an imperative to be secretive about nocturnal visitations. Yet it was the first exclusion from the membership of the club we had created in a de facto way and the trip lacked something as a result.

One week after our trip to Berlin I would see Jane and Sarah together again. The Duchess decided that she needed to visit Poland and scheduled a trip for her new flagship charity on 29 November. We were to have dinner with the Deputy Minister of Health and then proceed by mini-van to a number of orphanages in the countryside. This first charity trip to Eastern Europe would set the precedent for all of Sarah's future trips. The visit was structured around a particular problem involving children, and press coverage was maximised. The Duchess would later receive a great deal of criticism for the press coverage; her detractors would accuse her of controlling the press to enhance her image and even to profit financially. This is not the place to address these issues, except to say that Sarah was fighting for her life. She was going head to head with Princess Diana, who had honed manipulation of the press into an art form. Sarah was pitted against the shrewdness of Diana. Burdened with spontaneity and authenticity, Sarah never had a chance. It would take years before the futility of this competition became apparent and in late 1992 it was with a sense of hope that Sarah, accompanied once more by Jane, arrived in Warsaw airport.

When Sarah saw me she hurried over. We had been having a bit of trouble with our relationship and as an act of protest I had avoided attending the lavish Thanksgiving party she had just thrown. Sarah's hot-and-cold behaviour patterns were not limited to her relationships with staff and servants. She had a tendency to obsess upon a new friend, only to withdraw when the relationship became too serious or demanding. At this point in my relationship with the Duchess, she seemed to be distancing herself from me, and I was very upset with her.

'You missed such a nice party,' she began. 'We had a marquee put in the back of the house and I rented a Wurlitzer and had loads of American songs and all of your brother's favourite songs, and we danced and had such fun.'

'Sorry to have missed it, Your Royal Highness,' I replied formally.

'Oh, stop it! I am not such an ogre. I wrote you a letter that explains everything – please read it and then let's talk.'

I agreed and then went over to greet the other members of the group. To capture photo opportunities, Sarah had invited Robin Matthews (the photographer from the Victoria adventure) and to ensure my cooperation she had invited Stephanie as well. The old triangle was back in place.

We had a large number of rooms reserved for Sarah's growing entourage at the Marriott and a short time to check in and prepare for the Gala dinner party with government officials. Jane sought me out immediately and asked if she could meet me in my room. Thinking that our conversation on the train and our subsequent separation had taken the sting out of her obsession, I agreed. She entered the room carrying two letters. 'Allan, the Duchess wants you to read this,' she began as she handed me a voluminous envelope. 'Thanks,' I responded, opening it up and thinking that perhaps she would leave while I read it. 'She wants it back when you are finished, she said,' taking a seat and crossing her arms.

'What for?' I asked with surprise and a little anger.

'It is very personal and we need to shred it when you are finished.'

This was a first for me. I already had a number of letters, notes, photos and even signed collages from the Duchess and she had never spoken of security measures.

'Okay,' I replied, shaking my head.

The letter was over ten pages long and was filled with confused, emotional explanations about John being jealous of Sarah's closeness to me. It spoke of her feelings for John and her concerns about their relationship, asking me periodically for patience and help. She then spoke of the Victoria trips and how important they had been to her and enclosed her diary of the journeys. She had offered me her diary for two reasons: she hoped I could use it for our development of the book, but she also wanted me to see her early impressions and feelings about me and how she regarded me as 'a spiritual friend, the likes of which I will never lose', and her flattering comparisons of me to Prince Albert. She hoped this letter would correct my impression that she had lost her commitment to our relationship.

'You can keep Her Royal Highness's diary of the trips, but I do need to take the letter back.'

I handed it to the officious Jane, who seemed to be enjoying her role as secret courier. As I gave it back to her she handed me one of her own. 'Would you read this?' she asked. It was a three-page letter which pretty much encapsulated our conversation on the train and reiterated the points she made in the letter she had sent to my home. It said nothing new. 'We wrote these on the plane this afternoon,' she supplied. I waited for the next sentence and, believe it or not, she continued with: 'I must ask you for the letter back.'

'Of course,' I said solemnly. 'You are a married woman and probably need to destroy this.' She nodded her head, pleased with my understanding of her sensitive position, and took back the note.

'Jane, could you do me a favour?' I asked. And, as Jane typically would, she brightened up at the prospect.

'Of course,' she replied eagerly.

'I brought the Duchess a sixteenth-century icon from Russia and wanted to surprise her. Would you let me put it in her room when she is not there?'

This suggestion seemed to fill her with delight. It was a chance to be covert, to conspire with me, and for the cause of good. 'She is with Theo now — we could do it now,' she said. As Sarah's dresser, Jane had easy access to the Duchess's rooms. She would pack and unpack, mend the clothes and lay out the wardrobe and jewellery for the various events, so it was a simple matter to get in. Once in the Duchess's room, I was surprised to see that on her night table she had placed an enormous photo of the Duke. Later I would give her travelling frames for photos of Beatrice and Eugenie, but Sarah would never openly display a photo of John Bryan. Jane noticed my surprise and said, 'She always travels with that photo.' I thought that such a gesture spoke volumes, and I am glad that the couple now live under the same roof again.

I placed the gift and a note under Sarah's pillow and Jane and I departed the room. We had a short time to get ready for dinner. Jane seemed to have enjoyed this bonding experience and, as we separated, she brushed up close to me and said, 'Come to my room after dinner.' Clearly our previous conversations had had little effect on her current expectations.

Dinner was an annoying diplomatic affair, in which the Polish government tried to enlist Sarah's assistance without really articulating any plan for what they wanted her to do. The gala was filled with members of the press and with the new employees I had supplied for the Duchess. I watched with growing disdain as our Texan lawyer and his wife competed to court the Duchess. Jane had little chance even to catch her mistress's eye. As the evening began to break up, Stephanie told me her room number and I started saying my goodnights. Jane came over and, actually pushing me against the wall with her body, whispered, 'Come over in 15 minutes.'

'Jane, you have no idea how tired I am,' I replied, again hoping to avoid a direct confrontation.

'It will be worth it,' she teased. 'I will wake you up.' Despite her seductive words, this was not the Jane of Cap Ferrat. This was the old Jane, being insistent and shrill, not willowy and seductive. It was somehow disconcerting, as if she were out of costume and out of character, trying to rehearse a role she had once played but had now forgotten.

'Sorry,' I said resolutely, 'but we have to get up very early tomorrow.'

'All right,' she said in a small, very disappointed voice – a voice that had an edge.

I said my goodnights to the others and proceeded directly to Stephanie's room.

The short night went by too fast and this time there were no notes under the door. The next morning we met for a quick breakfast. Our plan was to drive off just at dawn. As I approached the buffet I sighted Jane, and she looked angry. She bounded over to me with a vengeful look and grabbed my arm.

'What is wrong?' I began, but she cut me off.

'I called you last night, you see . . .'

'Well . . .' I searched for the right words.

'You could have been straight with me, you know,' she continued.

'Look, Jane, I have tried . . .' Before I could finish, she released my arm and strode away with large, angry steps. That was the end of the conversation.

I found the Duchess and said, 'Ma'am, I am very sorry, but I need to get back to Frankfurt right away.' The Duchess rarely missed anything when it came to the personal interaction within her circle. 'I see,' she said with a sad smile.

When I spoke of the factors that precipitated the rejection stage of Sarah's relationship with Jane, I said they were threefold, and only named the first two. This was the third – Jane had become an emotional liability, which required too much of her mistress's time.

After breakfast the group mounted their mini-van and prepared to drive into the sunrise. I was very sad to take leave of them, but felt too enormous a sense of pressure and guilt. I recalled the parting in my diary of 30 November 1992:

What a hodge-podge of triangles – a geometric wonder. As I waved goodbye to a vanload of friends it was difficult to decide on whom to gaze. There was HRH beautifully dressed with a red blazer over a black turtleneck, smiling and waving at me with the renewed friendship of which she wrote in her long, stream-of-consciousness letter, which I was asked to return and destroy. Jane, hurt, sensitive, burning with love for me . . . Stephanie looking impish and fresh, despite hours of sweaty, hot sex and perhaps three hours of sleep . . .

Sad as it was, I felt that it would require such extreme behaviour to drive a stake through the obsession which consumed Jane. With sadness and regret, I watched my friends begin a new adventure without me. I knew that at some point along the way Sarah would reinforce the message I had just given by my forced absence.

And so Sarah and I, then, ended the first stage of our respective relationships with Jane. The second stage had begun. There would naturally be a transition, and times in which Jane's hopes would be rekindled, but clearly the period of resolute rejection had begun.

I followed the remainder of the trip by reading the reports from the tabloids. The day after the return of the Polish adventurers I was surprised when my secretary Anna announced with a quizzical look that Jane was on the phone. I was greeted by a very stiff voice which coldly greeted me with, 'Good morning, Her Royal Highness asked me to call you.'

'Did you have a good trip, Jane?' I asked.

'Her Royal Highness would like to speak to you,' she continued, without acknowledging my question.

'All right,' I replied.

'Would you call her, then?' asked Jane.

'You mean you called me just to ask me to call her?'

'That is correct,' confirmed the icy voice.

'Look, Jane, I can tell that you are . . .' Before I could even begin to say the next word, I was cut off by a mechanical voice which sounded like one of those computerised telemarketing calls, devoid of any semblance of humanity.

'She is expecting your call.'

'All right, Jane, I get it. Can you at least tell me what this is about?'

'Her Royal Highness needs to see you here tomorrow. It is very urgent.'

'I have language school in Switzerland tomorrow, for a whole week. It is impossible for me to see her.'

Now Jane got a little frightened. She must have thought that she could deliver this simple invitation in a manner that showed her anger, but did not calculate encountering resistance to her mistress's request. Her fear of relaying my refusal to the Duchess broke down the barrier of her pride.

'Allan!' she almost screamed. 'She really needs you. The publisher is getting her very upset and she has prepared a surprise party for all the people that worked on the book. She wants to have another Fireside Chat. Please, Allan, she really needs you.' Then, as an afterthought (and I must say this broke my heart) she added, 'Robin and . . . Stephanie will be here tomorrow night, and Her Royal Highness has reserved a room for you at the Royal Berkshire Hotel.'

'My goodness,' I thought. This is too much. Did the Duchess intend on Jane saying that? Was Jane meant to humiliate herself as an act of retribution for causing me to desert the team on the Poland trip? It was possible. I felt awful for Jane, realising how much that last line must have hurt. It was tantamount to forcing Jane to say that her mistress had set up a cosy love nest and supplied it with her competitor, then ask if I would come.

'I will call her,' I said quietly.

'Thank you!' burst out Jane with obvious relief.

The next day, at Romenda, it was clear that Sarah was feeling as if the individuals representing the distinguished publisher were patronising her though they would, I'm sure, be too professional to do that. At one point in the meeting, she asked me to leave the room with her and with Jane at her heels was barely able to close the door to her dining-room before bursting out in tears. 'They are shitting on me, Starkie,' she cried. 'They don't want me on the cover.'

'Do something, Allan,' pleaded Jane.

We were able to salvage the meeting and after the publishers departed I had about an hour alone with the two ladies before the guests began to arrive. Christmas was only three weeks away and John's gift had just arrived. During the Victoria trips Sarah had noticed the way that Victoria had designed secret gifts for Albert. As I have pointed out, we were very much under the spell of the great queen, so Sarah decided that she needed to create a Victorian gift for John and an equally intriguing present for Her Majesty the Queen.

She and Jane designed a sterling silver globe that opened in the centre to reveal a secret message, and contained a secret compartment to conceal photos of Sarah. The implied message was that John and Sarah might share the whole world one day. Jeweller Theo Fennell executed the design. Theo fitted into the Duchess's world. He had graduated from Eton and had the right social status and appearance. Tall, blond and good-looking, we would include him as a guest in many of our parties, and ultimately he would become Jane's employer. In fact, one of Thomas Cressman's last living acts would be to phone Theo to inform him that Jane was too ill to come to work (the Saturday before he was killed). One of the last things that Tim Kent did before discovering Thomas's body was to call Theo to see if he could locate Jane. It was as if fate had provided us with a macabre script which would unfold sometime in the future. We all had our parts, and we would all meet again to play our roles in the final act. But those sinister events lay hidden in the future and on this cheerful December afternoon the two ladies unpacked the globe with unconcealed excitement. When it emerged from its box it resembled a shiny silver football. One could not even be sure it was a globe at all. The two ladies stared in shared disappointment at the shiny ball.

'If we etched the oceans to make a contrast with the land it would look more like the earth,' I suggested.

'Exactly, Starkie!' exclaimed the relieved Duchess as she handed me the phone and dialled Theo's number, glaring at Jane all the while. In all fairness to Jane (who was sulking), I believe that the globe had been sent before she had had a chance to inspect the completed version.

After the diffusion of the explosively inappropriate globe, Sarah excused herself to go upstairs, leaving me with Jane. We were in a large room to the right of the house, which served as both sitting-room and study. It was a comfortable room with over-stuffed furniture and even an upholstered coffee table, and made one feel cosy and safe.

'I hope you have forgotten your anger with me, Jane,' I began.

'I am just very hurt and very disappointed,' she replied with shielded eyes.

· 'I am sorry, Jane. As I have told you, we need to let these other relationships run their course.'

'You are making a big mistake,' she said, then began to cry and ran out of the room. This type of behaviour would typify the rejection stage, which would last until the summer of 1993. Jane would become very upset or angry at any reference to her feelings for me. The unfortunate scene was interrupted by the arrival of Robin, Benita and Stephanie, who joined us for dinner. We reminisced about the trips and even planned a reunion during the Carnival in Venice the following February. Stephanie could detect the tension between Jane and me and resorted to communicating by scribbling notes on scraps of paper and passing them to me under the table. That is how paranoid Jane was able to make us feel about an otherwise healthy relationship.

After dinner we replayed our party games and retold our party jokes, then the Duchess passed out gifts that she had commissioned as keepsakes. Each of us received a Halcyon Box with the surface rendered in enamel to represent the map of the world. The top of the lid was painted to resemble a compass. On the inside of the lid there was an enamel inscription which read: 'Her Royal Highness, the Duchess of York – Travels'. It was a very thoughtful gift and we were all touched. It was prophetic that the boxes were made by Halcyon, for those journeys truly were halcyon days. There would be stormier weather ahead.

When I arrived at my home in Frankfurt the next day after the emotional visit, I was greeted by the Duchess's playful voice on my answering machine:

> Starkie, hello Starkie, hi Starkie. This is a really, really . . . oh, let's not say that . . . I am really, really pretty and I have big boobs and red hair, ooow. Fuck. Starkie, will you pick up the fucking phone? Hello, Allan, hi, it's the Duchess of York here. Just joking, I am making such nonsense, Starkie, listen. Thank you so much for yesterday, for flying all the way over and doing all the work and for working so hard on my book and for being such a little wonderful ball and I am very grateful, and thank you very much indeed . . . and Starkie, please don't worry, it was me who was upset yesterday . . . I didn't get upset with you, I felt vulnerable and threatened, and miserable . . .

It went on for many more minutes, as her messages always did, but you can see how charmingly provocative she was. She began the message with an imitation of an East End accent which then transitioned to her 'posh voice' when she announced that she was 'Duchess of York'. It was that type of cute behaviour which kept Jane and the rest of us virtually hypnotised. My personality was already formed, but Jane could not resist moulding herself after so charming a character. During the period of rejection Jane was only able to watch and imitate, for the Duchess was unwilling or unable to spend time instructing Jane in what was real and what was a façade. As a result, Jane's development was done without real guidance, and I believe that is where the damage began.

I used this particular message to show that the Duchess could often seem vulgar and overtly sexual. But in reality Sarah was neither of those things and, most of all, she was not promiscuous. The unguided and vulnerable mind of Jane was unable to distinguish between reality and artifice. She copied both, literally and with equal measure, within her own limited frame of reference. Jane was not privy to the intimate details of Sarah's private life. She had no way of knowing the prohibitions and limitations that her mistress imposed on the four romantic relationships (which happened consecutively, not all at once) that occurred during their years together. Jane had no real way of knowing where Sarah drew the line, and so she did not know that such boundaries existed, nor the difference between flirtatiousness and adultery. Jane was imitating an actress without knowing which lines were real and which memorised from the screenplay. The repercussions of this confusion would not become apparent until later, when Jane emerged from her cocoon.

CHAPTER EIGHT

PALACE CONFESSIONS

CHRISTMAS WAS RAPIDLY approaching and the holiday season has a curious way of forcing a person to reassess their life – and to think about how and with whom one wishes to start the New Year. For the Yorks it was to be a poignant and emotional time. It would be their first Christmas as a separated couple, and the first Christmas in which Sarah would be excluded from the major events of the royal household. The family celebrates the season with a series of parties at Buckingham Palace, reconvening in Sandringham for private celebrations and shooting. Naturally, the Queen wished to have her granddaughters by her side; yet the presence of the estranged Duchess posed a number of problems. It was decided that Sarah would be allowed to spend the time in Norfolk in a small farm outside the walls of Sandringham, called Wood Farm. She would dutifully dress and groom her daughters for the parties and events at the castle to which she personally would not be invited. It was reminiscent of the novel *Little Lord Fauntleroy*, in which the inflexible grandfather of a young lord forces the decent but unrecognised mother to live outside the walls of their grand estate, while the little lord is groomed for his future station. Sarah had never read the book, but got teary-eyed when I told her the plot.

To diffuse the stigma and suffering associated with this arrangement and also to show the solidarity and residual love shared by the couple, the Yorks decided to host a joint Christmas party at Buckingham Palace in early December, even sending out joint Christmas cards. The party was the first of a number of visits I would make to the palace, and the first opportunity I would have to witness the collective interaction of many of the protagonists of this story, all present at the same event. This would provide a number of startling revelations.

Sarah was so inundated with new employees, either lent to her from John and me or hired for her by us, that a great portion of the guest list seemed to read like that of my own company party. Naturally, John Bryan was not invited and it was a painful reminder of his exile that his partner and five of his employees would enter the very palace gates that would forever remain barred to him. On top of his past transgressions John had been exposed just four days prior to this party by an angry press. He had apparently tried to sell the name of Prince Andrew's new girlfriend to a tabloid for £20,000. The fast-talking Bryan had not realised that his negotiation was being taped and there was no way he could deny the deed.

I arrived early at the small guard booth that stands against those great, black, wrought-iron gates and, after the guards ascertained that my name was on the list, was allowed to enter the palace grounds. I was escorted to the façade that one sees from the Mall, through a portal on the right side of the palace, and then entered through a vestibule into a large ballroom called the Royal Cinema. It really is a cinema, in which the seats can be removed for parties.

The Duchess was standing at the door as I arrived and Jane was hovering close behind. 'Starkie!' Sarah bellowed and as I bowed she too bowed in fun and we bumped our heads. 'What is your brother up to?' she whispered.

'We left him in a Chinese restaurant and we will meet him after your party for dinner,' I replied.

'Poor fellow,' she said, shaking her head. 'Do be extra nice to him tonight. It must be awful for him. I hope he learned a lesson, though. Starkie, you cannot outsmart the press and your brother has to learn that.'

'Yes,' I agreed. 'He seemed a little depressed, but we will cheer him up later – it's sort of a company party.'

'That's for sure,' she giggled. 'Jim and Bethany were the first to arrive,' she rolled her eyes as she said that. Jim was the Texan lawyer we had given to Sarah, and Bethany was his wife. Sarah enjoyed sincere compliments but generally disliked somewhat flattering behaviour, and Bethany Hughes could sometimes be like that.

'Have you had a look round the palace?' asked the Duchess, as if such visitations were common occurrences.

'No, not yet.'

'Oh, you must!' she exclaimed. 'Where is that idiot?' she said, looking for Tony Blackmore, her butler. The Duchess would often use insulting endearments for her favourites, and Tony truly was one of her most loyal servants. In addition, he had been trained at the palace and had spent years as a footman to the Queen. Sarah now only had three servants who had worked in the palace and they were invaluable in maintaining her sense of credibility and link with the royal household. These people were Tony Blackmore, Jane Ambler and, of course, Jane Dunn-Butler.

Unable to locate Tony, the Duchess continued with: 'You still have a lot of time before everyone arrives. *Jane!*'

Never far from earshot, Jane approached reluctantly, followed by a balding man with a bushy moustache. He was fairly short and considerably older than she. 'I don't believe you have met Christopher,' she said quietly, with a tone of apology and some embarrassment. We shook hands and I felt a huge wave of relief that I had not slept with his wife. In fact, I felt very sorry for him. I do not mean to be cruel, but Christopher had the look of a beaten dog. I am not implying that Jane had beaten him; it seemed that life had done so. He stood with a straight and even rigid posture, yet he gave one the impression of being stooped and bent by a great burden. He seemed like a person who was aware that the world had somehow not been generous to him but was trying hard to keep his dignity, and somehow, that Herculean effort had exhausted him. This was no Heathcliff.

What I found very interesting was the manner in which Jane behaved around Christopher. I would see them together on other occasions in the future and I noticed an increasing tendency for Jane to become dismissive and impatient with her husband. On this particular evening her body language indicated that she did not even want to be associated with this man. They had virtually no eye contact and stood at least several feet apart. Jane was not rude to Christopher, she just seemed to consider him to be invisible.

We excused ourselves and Jane and Tony took turns showing me round the palace. Jane was considered the palace expert, as she was the only current member of the Duchess's staff that had actually lived there. In addition, Jane still spent a fair amount of time in the tiny office in which the Duchess maintained a palace presence and received fan mail.

Let me describe the inside of Buckingham Palace and my initial impressions of life within its walls. The Palace has about 600 rooms which are connected by a series of extremely long, wide corridors. It felt somehow as if it were simply another of those many castle-museums we had visited on our research trips and yet it is teeming with life, and still inhabited by a reigning monarch. I suppose Sarah and Jane might have argued that it was also inhabited by other monarchs, who no longer reigned or even breathed, and on that particular night I probably would not have disagreed. The corridors and vestibules seemed faded, like an etching of an old Victorian sitting-room. The carpets are red and in some cases well worn. The walls are papered in silk, mostly green fabric, and covered with oil paintings of the nameless faces and forgotten ships which once built and protected an empire. Stacked against the walls of these endless corridors is an army of dark cupboards and mahogany cabinets, standing silent guard over the dusty treasures of a fading past.

The most disconcerting thing about Buckingham Palace is that people *live* there. As I walked those spooky, empty corridors on that winter night, I would have been prepared to encounter ghosts. The fact that living people dwell in that tired place felt quite astonishing. For, as one regarded the doors that lined those decaying halls, small cards with the names of the royal occupants within the various suites could be discerned. On the second floor, the Yorks still maintained their apartment. It overlooked the front of the palace and on a more cheerful, summer day I would witness the changing of the guard from the inside of their flat. They had inherited the suite from Prince Charles, and Diana had even occupied it for a short while. It consisted of six rooms, all connected in a row – what we would call a railroad flat in America. To my mind that suite contained much more intimate charm than the sparse, empty ambience of Sunninghill Park and reflected more of the couple's personality. It was filled with massive furniture and yet was very cosy. Long, pleated curtains bracketed the tall windows that overlooked the Mall. In the sitting-room, the desk and tables were brimming with silver-framed photos of various members of the family, as if their very likenesses still carried a symbolic significance which was greater than just that of a family photo. These same images would appear on stoneware and lithographs and be purchased and treasured in the homes of millions of people. But here they were just pictures of parents and children. For those famous images are people too – people who, even in the inner sanctum of their family glory, live much like everyone else. That realisation, underscored by the abrupt transition from the institutional severity of the corridor to the human warmth of the apartment, was a strange revelation. It felt as if one were walking through the British Museum and, upon opening the wrong door, stumbled upon an exhibit that was still alive.

I remember my conversations with Jane about life within the palace. She had lived on a floor occupied by servants during the first two years of her employment. 'It is called the "dresser floor" and at first I lived there with the other royal dressers,' she explained. 'Her Majesty has two and the Princess Royal also has one.'

'Was Princess Diana's dresser living with you?' I asked, soaking up this royal trivia.

'Oh no, she is at Kensington Palace,' answered Jane with a slight smile of superiority at my foolish question. 'After a short time I was moved to the "hospital floor", just up there,' she motioned. 'That was a little nicer – we had a large kitchen and we would sometimes have little parties there.'

'Were you happy here?' I asked.

'No, Allan. I never felt at home,' she answered sadly. 'I was treated poorly by some of the other servants; they never were very friendly towards me, and as things got worse with Her Royal Highness they became horrible.'

'Why didn't you move out?' I asked.

'When I first starting working for the Duchess, Sunninghill Park was not yet completed and I couldn't afford to move out of the palace. I would be embarrassed to tell you how little I was paid – how little I am paid even now,' she confessed.

'But I thought it was a prestigious thing to work for the royal family.'

'It is,' she replied with a sardonic grin, 'that's why they do not feel it necessary to pay us very much.'

At the time of our conversation, I believe, Jane was earning about £10,000 a year. This made me even more aware of the relative cost of her extravagant gifts to me.

'Is that why you married?' I asked.

'I'd rather not answer that,' she replied, with a look of injured dignity, as if I had accused her of selling herself. To change the subject, I asked her how she had got the job in the first place.

'I answered an advertisement,' she said simply.

'Come on!' I chuckled in disbelief.

'Truly,' she insisted. 'I had just finished school and I read an anonymous advertisement and answered it. A few months later I received an invitation to come here for an interview. Her Royal Highness offered me the position.'

This was beyond belief. As it turns out, though, she was not teasing me. In actuality, she had got her job precisely that way. Later, when I was interviewed about the book I had written about my years with the Duchess, people like Andrew Morton would ask, 'How did you meet the Duchess?' and I would jokingly reply: 'By answering an anonymous ad', in continued amazement at Jane's strange turn of fortune. It was almost as though she had won a lottery someone else had lost. For, had she never seen that magazine or wanted to leave Grimsby so desperately, Thomas Cressman might still be alive.

During our final trip to Berlin (from which Jane had been excluded), Sarah had confided a number of strange, prophetic things to me. I thought it would be good to get Jane's opinion on them, so I began with a provocative statement.

'Well, I guess you might be living here again soon.'

'What do you mean?' she said, looking shocked, as if I meant she would be leaving Christopher.

'The Duchess told me in Berlin that her fortune-teller has predicted that Prince Charles would either die in another skiing accident or be passed over as monarch, and that the Queen will abdicate soon.'

'Yes, I had heard that prediction,' replied Jane. 'But what does that have to do with me living here?'

I thought it was interesting that Jane did not even doubt the veracity of such a prediction, but simply wondered why it might require her to move. At this point Jane's mistress was relying on a host of fortune-tellers and astrologers, and Jane had grown accustomed to making plans in accordance with their predictions.

'Well, it would mean that the Duke would become Regent, and the Duchess told me she would stand by him. That would mean they would be living here,' I explained

'Oh yes,' Jane replied with relief, 'but she would need ladies-in-waiting for that, not me.'

Well, I had confirmed what I needed to know. It was clear that Sarah truly did believe these predictions, and that Jane seemed well apprised of their consequences. I had wanted this information because Sarah had asked me to convince John that he needed to be patient as she delayed her divorce, since it would be 'the wrong thing' to leave the Duke at such a pivotal point in history. I wanted to see if Sarah really believed this, or was just trying to have me prepare John for a delay for another reason. It now seemed that either Sarah was sincere, or Jane was well briefed.

Changing the subject from court politics to a more personal tone, I asked: 'What would you have done if you hadn't found this job?'

'I suppose I would have done something in fashion. I can design clothes and sketch pretty well.' That gave me an idea. I wanted to do something nice for Jane, out of pity but also genuine affection, and now I began to develop a plan. Let me point out that the Jane who accompanied me that evening was certainly not the willowy blonde of Cap Ferrat, but neither was she the eager travelling companion and understudy to the Duchess. This was Jane the servant, Jane the dresser from the servants' quarters. There was nothing provocative about her behaviour. It was apologetic and politely subordinate. This must have been the Jane that existed prior to the research trips and the studied duplication of Sarah's charm. This was the girl from Grimsby. During the months of the period that I have categorised as the rejection period, this type of behaviour was typical of Jane. She was very accommodating, almost frantically eager to please, hungry for any words of kindness (or any attention at all) and she could execute the deepest curtsey anyone had ever seen. But there was also a subtext of deep resentment and a palpable sense of mounting frustration.

When we returned to the others the room had begun to fill up. A band began playing country and western music. Imagine the incongruity of that, after walking those strange Palace halls. The party was not formal, but I was shocked to see a guest arrive in exercise clothes. I recognised him as Josh, John Bryan's personal trainer. He was a strange fellow, and through John and then Sarah became a sort of royal fitness guru. I would run into him at a number of parties in the coming years and it began to dawn on me that he might be filling another need among the younger denizens within the world of the royal household. At that time I simply thought it was incredibly rude to come to a party dressed as he was, but it was good advertising and I suppose it paid off.

The guests were an eclectic group. Many of those invited had been friends of the Duchess prior to her marriage. Others were admirers of the Duke; in one case, a lady seemed as obsessed with Prince Andrew as Jane was with me. It was an odd party. I finally met the beloved Jane Ambler. She had been Sarah's favourite and was again to emerge as the dominant assistant in the Duchess's life, totally eclipsing our poor Jane. Jane Ambler is a short lady with cropped, blondish hair and a snub nose. She, too, is married to a Christopher – and so we had a pair of Janes and Christophers that night and for the ensuing years. The difference between the two Christophers is as dramatic as the difference between the two Janes. Christopher Ambler is handsome, well groomed, incredibly witty and a very powerful manipulator. Without ever seeking employment from the Duchess (as Christopher Dunn-Butler was soon to do), the self-confident Ambler would develop projects that the vacillating Duchess had shelved, and carry them to a fruition they would otherwise never have attained.

The room was filling up when suddenly all eyes turned to the entrance. Prince Andrew strolled in followed by his dog Bendix. What happened next was nothing less than an education in the art of brown-nosing. Many of the sycophants who had come expressly in the hope of ingratiating themselves with the Duke found themselves unable to win a moment of his attention, and so they resorted to lavishing their attentions on Bendix. This was too much. I watched elegant ladies and habitually aloof gentlemen on their hands and knees chasing Bendix round the dance floor, while pouring out endearments in babyish tones. I doubt if Bendix ever conceded to reward any of them with a knighthood; in fact, he seemed rather dismissive of this behaviour, to which he had apparently grown accustomed.

It was getting late and I was beginning to feel pressured about John sitting alone in the restaurant waiting for us. But before I could leave, the Duchess got up on a small stage at the end of the dance floor and announced that three couples would have to compete in a

Texas two-step. The band struck up some silly Texan tune and I was forced into the fray with a partner of Sarah's selection. As soon as this humiliation was over, I took leave of the Duke and tried to catch Sarah's eye to tell her we would be joining her exiled lover. She was continuously being spoken to by the tireless Texan wife of our new attorney.

'Looks like another female conquest,' I joked.

In a perfect imitation of a Texan drawl she responded: 'Oh, ya Royal Hah-ness, what will ah evah do with ya gone for three whole weeks?'

Sarah and I laughed for a few seconds, and then I told her we needed to catch up with John. 'Tell him I will see him later on tonight,' she whispered and pecked me on my check. I extracted my colleagues (in Bethany's case almost literally) and we joined a sad playboy waiting alone at an empty banquet table in an otherwise full and festive restaurant.

The following day we conducted our last Fireside Chat of 1992. It was a sad time because we would all be going our separate ways for the holidays. At the time we were considering leasing a large joint office to combine Sarah's activities, such as ASB Publishing and her charity offices, with a London office for John and me. We had chosen Chelsea Harbour, and were in the process of negotiating a lease that would allow us some terrific amenities, such as a private elevator to our suite of offices. These discussions naturally focused on personnel and who we would use for the joint enterprises. As I pointed out, Jane Dunn-Butler had fallen out of favour at this period and I was determined to see that she was at least treated fairly. John disliked her and felt that she was an unnecessary expense. One of the ideas we had been developing for producing much-needed revenues for the Duchess was the establishment of a Duchess of York photo library, where the copyright for her photos could be guarded and billed as they were used internationally.

'That would be a great job for Jane,' I suggested.

'She is an idiot and would fuck it up,' replied John.

'Be respectful,' warned Sarah. 'But your brother has a point – Louise Dyer would be better suited for that.'

'Okay,' I agreed, 'but you said that you wanted to store your wardrobe in our suite of offices, didn't you?'

'Yes, Starkie,' replied Sarah, 'it takes up a lot of room and is very valuable, and also it would be nice if I could have a dressing-room there so that I could dress for events in London.'

This gave me the opportunity to suggest the idea I had formed while in the palace. 'We would need to inventory your wardrobe and insure it if we were leaving it in an unattended office.'

'Quite right, Starkie. Most of it came as gifts from Her Majesty and my wardrobe is the only valuable thing I have.'

'Well, wouldn't it be a great opportunity to make a book about your wardrobe?' I began. 'Jane could sketch each outfit and write a small synopsis of where you wore it, who attended and what happened. Jane sketches dresses really well . . .'

We brought Jane into the dining-room and presented the idea. 'Oh, Your Royal Highness!' she exclaimed, almost swooning. 'I would love to do that.' I offered to help and to credit the authorship to both the Duchess and Jane, as long as Jane was able to split the royalties with the Duchess. For the next six months I do not think a week went by without me reminding either Jane or Sarah about the project. Needless to say, we never really leased those offices and yet that was no reason not to produce that book. Jane simply seemed not to care. In my opinion she was too lazy.

On the other hand Jane had developed a side business of her own. She had discovered a costume jewellery manufacturer called Cabouchon and decided to sell their products. At first she targeted the servants at the palace and in Romenda Lodge, and ultimately even managed to get the Duchess to purchase some of these articles. It was not very lucrative and I always wondered why she did it. In retrospect I think that she felt it was a good way to meet people and create new acquaintances. Oddly, her last job would be with a jeweller, albeit of a more upmarket calibre.

In light of her poorly compensated efforts as a door-to-door saleswoman (even if they were Palace doors), I was very disappointed with Jane's lack of follow-through on the opportunity I had offered her. I have often said that Jane was ambitious, but the manner in which she tried to achieve her goals did not include even attempting one of the few projects for which her meagre education had actually prepared her. Jane did not want to be known as a fashion author, or a dress designer – she wanted a quicker road to success and social acceptance, and that road was lined with a series of men, not with time-consuming projects.

The year 1992 was mercifully drawing to an end. It was a year in which the monarchy was besieged by a host of tragedies ranging from fire to scandal, a year that Her Majesty would call her 'annus horribilis'. The next year would be filled with many new surprises and some extraordinary adventures for all of us. A new phase was to begin in Jane's life, and even in Christopher's. We exchanged gifts and wished each other well. It would be three weeks before we would reconvene and see what the New Year would bring us.

CHAPTER NINE

THE RESURRECTION

FOR SARAH AND JANE the next year would be one of great contrasts: motion and stagnation; scaling great mountains then falling into valleys of deep despair; crying out for freedom, while clinging to the confining ruins of the past. It was to begin with disappointment and would end with uncertainty.

Sarah managed to swallow her pride and endure the lonesome exile that had been imposed upon her during the holidays. She travelled to that obscure Norfolk farmhouse pathetically clinging to the magnificent gift she had commissioned for the Queen. It was a sterling silver cylinder to hold the royal tealeaves, forged by Jane's future employer Theo Fennell. The lid was crowned with a small seated corgi with his head slightly tilted, as if he were listening to his mistress's voice. Along the rim was a lovely inscription etched in the Duchess's own handwriting. In return, she was to receive a perfunctory gift that was not even properly wrapped. Sarah patiently endured all such slights and indignities with a stoic patience that I saw as courageous.

Jane's holidays were less than regal. She visited the parents from whom she was progressively distancing herself, in the northern town she wished to forget. Her brief but decisive interlude as Sarah's close confidante had temporarily ended and Jane was just another royal servant taking a respite for the Christmas holidays. She had experienced the intoxicating thrill of being a friend to the Duchess and an inside observer of the intrigues of palace life, and she longed to re-establish her personal link with the Duchess.

The year began with each lady having a clear agenda. Sarah wanted independence and financial success, and was more inclined to a divorce. Jane wanted to taste once more the power of being a member of Sarah's inner circle. The next 12 months would see Sarah fail sadly in her goals, while Jane would ultimately realise hers.

In the early months of 1993, however, Jane had no way of anticipating her success. On the contrary, the Duchess treated her more dismissively and complained about her performance. The period of rejection that had begun in November was continuing with unabated intensity; in fact, at times it appeared as if Jane might not keep her position.

Without the opportunity to accompany Sarah on the relationship-bonding trips of the past, Jane was forced to rely on the limited interaction she was offered within the walls of the small house. To further complicate matters, she developed a somewhat rare illness at about this period, an ovarian disorder which resulted in mood swings and growing bouts of depression. Now, in addition to her typical shrill cries for attention, Jane displayed a growing listlessness and lethargy, and a depressive nature.

Jane's reaction to setbacks, as I had already witnessed, was not pleasant. She was not a passive sufferer of disappointments. Although she maintained a strict sense of protocol and an ostensibly accommodating manner, she could become shrill, pushy and annoying. As the early months of 1993 progressed, Jane was excluded from the growing activity and excitement that surrounded the creation of Sarah's charity and business activities. She did not take this well and would make any attempt possible to interrupt our meetings, often creating disruption when she meant to simply gain attention. At one point during a meeting in February, Jane came running into the dining-room, curtseyed and cut John off, mid-sentence, to announce, 'Your Royal Highness, we are out of toilet paper.'

The obsessiveness of Jane's search for re-acceptance was not lost on the Duchess, who became increasingly annoyed. I believe that Jane's job performance often suffered when she was in such a frantic state of obsession. There were a number of examples of mistakes during this period, but the most sensational involved her simple tasks as dresser in preparation for an expedition to Mount Everest.

Sarah loves the mountains and she needed to undertake an

adventure that might help her to regain her sense of self-respect, which had been greatly damaged over the last several years. Sarah did most things in her life on a grand scale: when she married it was to the son of the Queen, when she strayed it made international headlines. And so, when she decided to climb a mountain, it would have to be Mount Everest. Perhaps sensing that even this daunting task might be beneath the Homeric proportions of her drive, she decided to bring a contingent of disabled persons with her – almost like an Olympic sprinter wearing ankle weights during the finals.

The goal was to reach the first station without the aid of oxygen, and Sarah kindly included me on the team. I was forced to decline, as the expedition would take over 30 days.

Naturally, there was a large amount of purchasing and packing of equipment associated with such a journey, and Jane was involved in organising the Duchess's luggage. I should point out that Sarah had been suffering from huge bouts of depression and had recently discovered the fashionable anti-depressant Prozac. She was so pleased with the effects of the drug that she encouraged many of her friends and relatives to try it. She lent me a book called *Listening to Prozac*, but warned, 'It prevents one from having an orgasm.' I was a little sceptical about such a costly solution but agreed to read the book. 'I could give you some tablets,' the Duchess offered eagerly. 'I had given a package to my father, but they made him violently ill.' I later developed a strong dislike for Major Ferguson as a result of a number of things he did to his daughter – not least among them publishing his book *The Galloping Major*, and providing Leslie Player with such a bounty of revelations about his intimate life that she could also write a book. But at this point all I could do was laugh at the thought of that tall, arrogant man, with his absurdly bushy eyebrows, puking Prozac all over the place.

The Everest expedition was the first long trip Sarah was to undertake without me as chaperone since the South of France photos had been published. On top of the geographical separation, telephone communication was not possible from the mountain – so it was almost four weeks after we had said goodbye that I received a call from my adventurous friend. She called from Katmandu in a state of great excitement. 'I did it, Starkie! I made it, and without oxygen,' she bubbled. 'And guess what? I am off Prozac!'

I had read the book she had given me and had been somewhat

negative about her reliance on this drug, so I happily responded, 'I am so proud of you.'

'Don't be,' she announced conspiratorially. 'Stupid Jane forgot to pack it – but we needn't tell that to your brother. Besides, I am quite looking forward to a good orgasm when I get back!'

Jane's forgetfulness had struck a blow for unmediated mental health and unimpaired sexual release. It was not to be the last time that this trait would create explosive side effects. Just two years later, Jane would be labelled by the world press as the dresser who lost the diamond necklace given to Sarah by the Queen. But Jane somehow managed to survive these transgressions, and in this case even to create a happy ending, for Sarah discontinued her use of Prozac with its unfortunate limitations.

As an aside, Sarah returned from the Himalayas with more than just a renewed sexual appetite. She also brought a souvenir. The Sherpa guide who had accompanied her was so enthralled with Sarah's charm that he volunteered his services to her, and she brought him back to Romenda Lodge. His name was an unpronounceable guttural sound that we decided to simplify and dubbed him Yeltsin. In harmony with the often-strange assignments that the ever-fluctuating staff were given, it was decided that Yeltsin (who spoke virtually no English) would answer the telephones. I always felt that Yeltsin's performance as receptionist somehow benefited Jane, for this truly was a case of the one-eyed man being king in the land of the blind. Yeltsin's almost comical role as telephonist, and his later attempts at mastering other Western skills, provided more than just comic relief. Jane, with Palace-trained protocol, seemed more solid and reliable in comparison. When Yeltsin finally bade a tearful farewell to the Duchess, he told the press that she was not just his friend but also 'his god'. As I say, Sarah did have a way of winning people over.

Despite Jane's perennial mistakes, and the added annoyance of her demands to be noticed, a strange conjunction of events was about to unfold that would allow her to rise from the lugubrious depths of her rejection and emerge in an even more important role in the life of her employer.

Sarah was achieving a good deal of media success with her charity Children in Crisis. After the Poland trip we had used the majority of 1993 to visit dismal orphanages and decrepit children's hospitals in desolate places like Albania. We always brought a contingent of journalists and tried to cooperate with them. Princess Diana was still the great favourite, but Sarah was slowly picking up ground, on the charity front at least. The press had been particularly kind when reporting on our trip to Albania, calling her 'the Duchess of Mercy', and Sarah was beginning to feel that she might be able to regain some of the lost public esteem she had enjoyed in her early years of marriage.

To support the Eastern European trips we would hold elaborate charity balls in London attended by important industrialists like Richard Branson. The accessibility and influence of such a successful businessman began to convince Sarah that other options existed for developing her business interest other than the fast-talking but non-producing Bryan. For in less than two years of financial independence, Sarah's overdraft was increasing at a startling pace. This terrified her, and did not seem to please the patient but increasingly demanding royal bankers. As the year progressed, each Fireside Chat brought another change in direction for the future of Sarah's business and marital plans. The message became increasingly clear that she did not plan on merging her interests with those of John, who remained controlling and was often verbally abusive.

Finally, towards the beginning of the summer, a very pivotal event took place at one of the chats. Sarah had spent some time preparing a handwritten document of perhaps two pages, which she brought sheepishly to the meeting.

'What do you have there?' asked John, peering over at the paper with a bemused look.

'I wrote a business plan,' said the Duchess tentatively but also with a degree of pride.

'Oh, Linky, how cute!' burst out the patronising Bryan. 'Let me see . . . oh, her first business plan . . . let's hang it up on the refrigerator next to Eugenie's crayon drawing!' he exclaimed, actually getting up to walk to the adjacent kitchen.

It was Sarah's first real attempt at taking control of the meetings which had typically been dominated by John. It was Bryan's almost mesmerising control of the Duchess that had prompted *The Times* to label him as 'Fergie's Rasputin'. The insensitivity of John's reaction sent Sarah running into the garden with tears in her eyes.

I waited about five minutes and then went out to the garden to console her. There I found her sitting on a bench next to Jane. It was a surprise – Jane had not even been in the room when the incident occurred. Apparently, the moment Jane sensed a sob, she had automatically launched herself like a cruise missile in the direction of the Duchess's favourite bench. They were seated inches apart, sobbing softly together, with Jane stroking the Duchess's arm. I could hear Jane whispering soothing words in the calming tones usually reserved for an injured child.

As Sarah was taking her first steps towards freeing herself from the yoke of John's dominion over her, the press coincidentally renewed their campaign of discrediting him. In an article written during this period, the press posed the timely question: 'Is this man leading her to disaster?' Sarah's already diminishing confidence in John was further eroded and I was awoken one morning by her pleading words into my answering machine, which I began to believe was sharing an even more intimate relationship with the distressed Duchess than I was:

> Starkie, it's your aunt, your very sick aunt from England. I've gone downstairs and it's half past, uh, I don't know what time it is, about eight o'clock, nine o'clock your time and it's Saturday morning and I'd really like to talk to you. I am . . . hopeless [said in a whisper]: this morning, in big headlines, 'Is this man leading her to disaster?', can he do more damage? We need to do damage limitation now, and I really do need to talk to you because we need to *change* all this so we can get it right.

Sarah's plan for 'change' was to create an infrastructure of her own loyal followers, which would enable her to pursue opportunities without the direction and interference she had experienced from John.

On 6 August Sarah was ready to implement this change and Jane was to be the direct beneficiary – and, perhaps in an odd way, the first victim. We conducted a Fireside Chat to which a host of outsiders were invited. The attendees included Sarah's re-hired assistant Christine Gallagher, a chartered accountant named Jeremy Scott (whom I had introduced to Sarah), a second Texan lawyer we had hired and lent to Sarah, and Jane Dunn-Butler, not in search of toilet paper this time, but as a participating member.

The meeting began with John strolling into the dining-room in his velvet slippers with embroidered helicopters and squash rackets (a Jane and Sarah original). His mouth was filled to capacity with M&Ms, but he managed to sputter, 'Sure are a lot of people here – is this a Fireside Chat or a tag-team wrestling match?'

'Please sit down,' said a staid Duchess.

'Should we begin with your new business plan?' asked John, making a poorly timed reference to the last disaster.

'That's enough, John, we will begin by Jeremy summarising the accounts.'

'Well, ma'am,' began the studiously serious accountant, 'the total overdraft has reached £245,000 with an additional £96,000 in unpaid creditors, and £30,000 owed by your publishing company.'

'What does that mean, Jeremy?' asked the frightened lady with a royal title, two princesses to support and virtually no income.

'It means that at your current rate of expenditure you need about £35,000 a month to break even.'

This was a frightening thought. With the exception of selling the rights to a Budgie cartoon series, and the meagre revenues from the Victoria book, little had been done to augment Sarah's tiny income. The Duke was as generous as he could afford to be, but his contribution was too small to make an impact on the expenditures currently being incurred by the Duchess.

'All right, Jeremy,' said a bored and impatient Bryan. 'What about the joint offices, Sarah, are we going to sign a lease?'

'For the time being there will be no joint offices,' responded the now resolute Duchess. 'And I have decided to create my own staff. Christine will now be a project manager and Jane will be my assistant accountant.'

This was fantastic – I mean truly unbelievable. Looking over at the two newly minted business ladies, I realised that they had been well prepared for this meeting. Jane was dressed in a business suit and was jotting down every word on a yellow legal pad. Her Alice in Wonderland hair band was firmly in place and her face, meticulously painted with what she must have deemed to be Wall Street understatement, was pinched in concentration. When the announcement of her promotion was made, she looked up from her pad with a slight smirk on her face. As our eyes met I realised that her face had contorted into a strange sneer – a distorted look of triumph. I would see that strange look again, exactly the same look of triumphant loathing, but in a decidedly different context.

If my reaction were one of surprise, John seemed aghast and amused at the same time. He began to laugh as if he thought it were a joke, then looked first at Christine and then at Jane with a stare of complete disbelief. From that point onward the room shifted into two competing camps: the followers of John and the new staff of the Duchess of York. As a sign of protest John devoted the remainder of the meeting to ignoring the discussions that followed, while scribbling a new version of the words to his favourite song on a scrap of paper. He would periodically elbow me in the ribs to call my attention to a particularly funny line as he wrote:

'I Did It Her Way'

And now the divorce is near,
And so I face the final curtain.
Although the tears subside,
I find it still so uncertain.
To think, I did all that,
In a very shy way,
Oh yes, oh yes, I did,
I did it,
Her way.

Regrets, I've had a few,
But then again, too few to mention,
I did what she told me to,
And saw it through,
At my expenses.

She planned each chartered course,
Each careful step along the buy-way,
But more, much more than this,
I did it her way.

For what is a man?
What has he got?

If not his balls,
Then he has not.

To say the things,
She likes to hear,
To do the things,
That reduce my fear,
The overdraft shows,
I loved the blows,
And did it,
Her way.

As the lyrics indicate we had reached a point of some frustration.

We limped through the remainder of the meeting, trying to divide the existing projects among the newly created staff. Jane was to retain her duties as dresser, but, starting that day, she was to become much more. As a dresser Jane had clearly been a servant; now, in the comparatively elevated rank of accountant, she had risen to a different level. This change was not simply titular. In actuality Jane would be able to broker her new position into an enormous increase in her influence. In the past Jane had been privy to a host of royal secrets. To this she was now able to add the financial secrets of her mistress. Jane would be one of the very few people in the Duchess's world who would have access to virtually the full range of Sarah's activities. The bond of trust that was forged that day would link the two ladies for the rest of their lives. It is hardly a wonder, then, that in her moment of greatest distress Jane would call upon her ex-mistress — but what did Jane want from Sarah so shortly after Cressman bled his life away?

On that warm August day in 1993, however, we could not predict the strange effect that this promotion would have on Jane. The period of rejection had abruptly ended and she was drawn more closely than she could ever have anticipated into the inner circle of Sarah's life. The new Jane, the *resurrected* Jane, would immediately begin to demonstrate a new persona. Her dress, mannerisms and even her speech patterns and accent would change dramatically. The timid girl from Grimsby would soon become a newly minted Sloane Ranger. The months of resentment suffered during the rejection had put an edge on this new Jane. She was not willing to allow for the possibility of another defeat. What would emerge from the cocoon in which she had weathered her period of disfavour was to be a calculating, sexual predator, with mock-royal manners that soon would alienate other members of the group. Jane Dunn-Butler had ceased to exist. The Duchess was one of the first to notice the change, and chose a title for the stranger who had appeared in our midst. Henceforth, the new entity that occupied the shell of the former dresser from Grimsby would be known as Lady Jane.

John flew to meet me in Frankfurt shortly after this pivotal meeting, to plan our reaction to these developments. Naturally, his agenda was clear. He wanted to regain total control of Sarah's life and keep that control until he manipulated her into saying 'I do'. He arrived in his usual state of enthusiasm – as if he had not just received a huge setback.

'Are you not concerned that we have just been pushed out of Sarah's affairs?' I asked, dumbfounded by his blasé attitude.

'Absolutely not. This is the best thing that could have happened,' he replied with one of those John Bryan grins which implies that he already has all the answers. 'Don't you see? With morons like Jane working for her, she is bound to fail miserably and she will be drawn right back to us; she will need us more, and if we play hard to get she will beg us to take control of her life.'

Now, he did have a point and, as it turned out, he was partially correct. We withdrew the majority of the support staff we had provided. Our second Texan lawyer was encouraged to leave, John's secretary and mine reduced their assistance to a minimum, and we allowed Jeremy Scott to work directly on the Duchess's payroll on a part-time basis. Lady Jane reported to Jeremy for the accounts and still had direct access to Sarah by virtue of her other more servile duties. Most importantly, as accounts-payable clerk Jane controlled the purse strings of the Duchess. It would not be long before she recognised the power this would offer her.

John's prediction began to be realised. Sarah's overdraft began to run way out of control. As the debt increased, the interest payments naturally became increasingly higher, and Sarah was becoming suffocated by debt without a hope of repaying the principal. As her overdraft mounted, her level of terror rose. John and I still carried on our Fireside Chats with Sarah, but his agenda had changed. Instead of suggesting new projects, he sabotaged the existing ones and discouraged proposed plans. The result was obvious. Sarah was stuck in the doldrums. She could not move forward – all she could do was continue to bleed money that she had little hope of repaying.

Lady Jane was by her side, tallying the bills and trying to juggle and delay the payments. It was often Jane who had to make the difficult choices of who simply not to pay and, naturally, Sarah was confronted with the bleak repercussions that these choices would cause. It got to the point where Sarah would be afraid to look at the screen of the automated bank machine when it dispensed cash – afraid to see the balance. Jane would become responsible even for withdrawing and transporting the petty cash.

By virtue of her control of the priorities of payment, Lady Jane wielded great power with the Duchess's suppliers, as well as within Romenda Lodge. Creditors were aware that Jane could decide when they would be paid and gave her the prestige and respect necessary to protect their livelihood. Among the staff, Lady Jane could decide when expenses would be reimbursed. For example, Sarah took to using her butler's mobile phone. At about this time the story broke that Princess Diana had been doing a little telephone stalking using her own phones. Sarah became more conscious of telephone security and ran up large bills on her butler's phone. Naturally, she planned on paying these bills, but Lady Jane procrastinated with processing the reimbursement, partially due to a feud between herself and the butler. And so, to the worlds both inside and outside the walls of Romenda Lodge, Lady Jane began to develop a reputation for being the one you had to please if you wished to be paid.

Despite Lady Jane's attempts at managing the cash, Sarah's financial situation was rapidly deteriorating and the staff was not equipped with the expertise to extricate her. Ironically, when under the most extreme financial stress the Duchess was more inclined to spend more. She did not spend much on herself, and made do with her old clothes and no new jewellery. But she wasted huge amounts of money on other people. Her two forms of financial extravagance lay in hiring extra staff, and in paying for the services of fortune-tellers, astrologers and other fashionable gurus. Diana shared the same preoccupation with such forms of rented solace and the two would spend hours discussing the various predictions.

At about this point Sarah was coming under the influence of a psychic who claimed to be in communication with the dead. I am still not certain how this lady was able to orchestrate such strange events, but rather amazing things began to occur in Sarah's home. A candle would fly out of its holder and Sarah would cry, 'Hector is in the room with us!'* At one point while on the phone with her new psychic, Sarah was looking at a small brass mantle clock that Prince Charles had given her. The soothsayer seemed aware of this and said 'Captain Lindsey is in contact with you and he will make the clock stop right now.' According to Sarah's disjointed call to me minutes later, the clock actually did stop.

Lady Jane had the opportunity of either witnessing these events or having the amazed Duchess re-tell the stories. Jane never doubted their veracity. It was amazing to see how literally she seemed to accept these events.

What was so pitiful about this situation is that these phenomena served as a distraction from the reality of how terribly Sarah's life was deteriorating. It provided false hopes from intangible forces, when no pragmatic solutions were sought for the actual problems facing her on a daily basis. Magic had become an opiate and Sarah allowed herself to fall under its spell.

———

By this point Sarah had amassed a staff of 13 people. There was no clear hierarchy among them, and no clear boss. As a result Sarah managed each servant individually, while the daily chaos of her household further sapped her strength and time. Lady Jane had elevated herself above the chaotic mêlée of the domestic world. Her new position had raised her status to that of a staff assistant. Nevertheless, she gave virtually no assistance in running the household and mediating the complex interpersonal and performance issues that arose daily from the unmanaged staff.

'Help me, Starkie,' pleaded Sarah, finally, as she began to sense the futility of her situation.

'Let's start off with dividing your life into three compartments: charity, business and private. Each category should have a department head so that only three people would report to you.'

'What about your brother?' she asked in the tone of a person

---

* Meaning the spirit of polo legend Hector Barrantes, the Duchess's deceased stepfather.

about to look over their shoulder to catch a glimpse of the nemesis that has been trailing them.

'This advice could have come from anyone,' I answered.

We began by asking each of the staff to write up a job description, which would allow us to make choices about who to retain. I would write formal job descriptions, using the information, for the few people we would wish to retain. The responses were often comical and ranged from eloquent missives that chronicled heroic, but poorly rewarded efforts, to pitifully terse, misspelled fragments describing the duties of picking up dog droppings from the garden. As I collected these documents I realised that only one employee had neglected to write one.

Lady Jane seemed hurt and somewhat irate when I asked for her job description. 'Allan, really!' she began. 'I do think that my duties are well known to Her Royal Highness.'

'Yes, Jane – so are everyone else's – nevertheless, we need to get it all down on paper and determine what is essential and what we can live without.'

The implication that anything Jane did was not essential seemed to be more than she could bear.

'If the Duchess feels that she needs to discuss the nature of my duties, I would hope she would ask me herself.'

That was the end of it. I still have those manilla envelopes overflowing with a strange collage of descriptions, which is reminiscent of Kipling's story about three blind men describing an elephant, for when they are read together it seems as if the employees are describing working in very different households. But from that pile of memorabilia, there is one description notable by its absence – a description of the duties of Lady Jane.

When I presented this information to Sarah she seemed saddened by the degree of confusion. 'Look,' I tried to explain, 'let's simplify it by hiring a senior housekeeper, and she can be the bad guy and fire all the non-essential people.'

'Oh no! I cannot be seen to be down-scaling now, not with all this uncertainty – not until after the divorce.'

'But we are paying a fellow and his wife to pick up dog shit!' I exclaimed.

'Well, someone has to do it,' replied the now angry Duchess.

'Yeah, but that is all he seems to do!'

'This is very distressing. I have an idea . . .' And then it began; yet another twist to the saga of Jane's strange involvement in the Court of Fergie. The idea was to hire the now unemployed Christopher Dunn-Butler to be a 'cost engineer'. Little Romenda Lodge was already overflowing with servants and staff – and to reduce the costs, we would hire yet another person!

So, shortly after the elevation of Lady Jane, the royal household greeted another Dunn-Butler. Christopher joined Sarah's staff and, in cooperation with Jeremy and Jane, attempted to find ways of reducing costs without a drastic reduction in staff. As the logic of this conundrum should have portended, Christopher had little success; in fact, the overdraft was completely out of control and growing at over £1 million per year.

The dynamics between Jane and Christopher, now colleagues, was awkward. Lady Jane appeared even more dismissive of her commoner husband than she had been when I first met him the previous Christmas. She seemed to want to avoid associating with him in front of the other members of Sarah's team, and restricted the contact to business-oriented issues.

At the same time the other Jane and Christopher, the Amblers, had also been taken, as a couple, into the world of the Duchess. Sarah had developed the idea for a new set of cartoon characters which she hoped might re-create the success she had enjoyed with Budgie. She called it 'The Patch'. The characters were a group of different types of vegetables that all lived together on the same patch of land. The vegetables came from different ethnic and social groups. I was very negative about this idea and received equally negative feedback from our literary agent. Nevertheless, the Amblers offered to develop the project on their own time, as partners.

This example summed up the difference between the two couples. Despite Lady Jane's promotion, and her excessive attempts at achieving a higher social standing, she remained timid about her roots. Her husband did not have a strong personality, and was inept at demonstrating charm during social events. The couple interacted poorly together, and just did not seem to fit. The Amblers, on the other hand, managed to behave as a team. Self-confident and humorous, they were able to achieve a more equal sense of friendship and partnership with the Duchess. As a result, the Amblers eclipsed the Dunn-Butlers, both socially and professionally.

I can vividly remember the Freddy Krueger and wicked-witch costumes the Amblers wore one year to a fancy-dress Hallowe'en party at Romenda Lodge, yet I could not even begin to remember how Lady Jane and *her* Christopher were dressed. They were unable to compete with the Amblers, and in a fairly short time Christopher Dunn-Butler left the Duchess's service. It was then that the rumours began.

CHAPTER TEN

LADY JANE: NEW YORK SOCIALITE AND JET-SETTER

LADY JANE AND CHRISTINE had flown ahead to New York and ensconced themselves in the luxurious Carlisle Hotel, while Sarah and I finished our gruelling trip to Bosnia. Our charity work had taken Sarah and me to some depressing places, but Bosnia was in a league of its own. Ethnic cleansing was still ongoing at this point in February of 1994, and we visited children's wards where infants had been shot in the groin so that if they survived they would be sterile. It seemed as if hate oozed through those dirty, oppressive streets, and virtually everyone we met was consumed with rage. Professors from the medical university told us, 'Serbia will not be cleansed until the last drop of blood is spilled from the Serbian pigs.' Even a top police officer bragged to me that he had relished killing Serbs with his bare hands. By the third day we were depressed and exhausted.

We had flown over on a cargo plane that dripped condensation onto the row of seats that had been bolted in the back to accommodate us. The thought of taking this same plane all the way to New York was somewhat daunting. Sarah and I were spending the last night in a dingy hotel in Split, Bosnia. Our rooms were at the end of a long hallway and directly across from each other. As I crossed over to visit Sarah after we returned from dinner, I noticed that a Bosnian bodyguard had been placed in the hallway directly between our rooms. An armchair had been moved to the hall and he sat on it with his machine-gun in hand. It was already late when I passed him and I noticed that his head was bobbing as he tried to stay awake.

I knocked and then entered the room, noticing that the door had not been locked. Sarah was sitting on the edge of her bed, looking completely worn out. 'Do you really want to spend 20 hours in that horrible cargo plane?' she asked.

'No,' I replied, 'I thought it was your idea.'

'Well, I say fuck them, Starkie. Let's fly Concorde!'

In a flash I was on the phone to BA and had managed to book a flight on Croatian Airlines to connect with Concorde in Heathrow. I would be flying with my new wife, Sarah Starkie.

When I left the Duchess's room I was so tired I did not even remember that the door had been unlocked when I had arrived. As I crossed the hall to my room I noticed that the armchair was vacant. It did not register that something might have been wrong. As it turned out, the bodyguard had disappeared and someone tried to get into the Duchess's room. As the door began to open she threw herself against it, fell to the floor and simply waited in terror, with her weight against the door, until the intruder left. Bosnia was not a pleasant place in 1994, and we were very relieved to board a normal aeroplane the next morning.

We arrived early enough at the Hounslow VIP suite at Heathrow for Sarah to call Princess Diana and brief 'Dutch' on the outcome of our recent adventures and her brush with disaster the night before. We boarded Concorde and immediately began our ritual of gin and tonics. Concorde is overrated in terms of service, but it is fast, and it was an odd feeling to start the day in war-torn Bosnia and descend onto the snowy, but safe, streets of New York with the sun still shining.

Lady Jane and Christine managed to drag themselves away from the plush salons of The Carlisle to meet us at the airport. My business partner, Bill Simon, was hosting us. Bill has sadly passed away, but he was a man of some influence in his time. His accomplishments included being Secretary of the Treasury for both Presidents Nixon and Ford, and then becoming a self-made billionaire. Bill had become acquainted with John Bryan's father during the days when Kissinger was secretly opening trade relations with China. During those tense Cold War adventures they had become great friends, and Simon joined the partners of our firm Oceonics.

Simon had provided the accommodation at The Carlisle for this eclectic trip, in which we would try to combine a host of business and charity meetings into a five-day visit. In his eagerness to be a generous host, Bill had hired a fleet of stretch limousines and a small army of bodyguards for the duration of our stay. At the head of this formidable force stood Lady Jane, waving her hand daintily at us as we exited the gate. She was extremely well dressed, and very relaxed around the Duchess. Curtseying deeply she said, 'Welcome, Your Royal Highness, I hope you had a good flight.' Sarah and I had consumed so many gin and tonics as we mapped out her life and made our 'Concorde confessions' that Jane's ludicrously banal greeting seemed awfully funny, and we both began to laugh. 'The Carlisle is beautiful, and you have a wonderful suite, ma'am,' Jane continued, choosing to disregard our irreverence for the formality of the greeting party. We were introduced to our head of security and a contingent of his guard force. They were off-duty New York police officers, one of whom was a very attractive but somewhat streetwise young lady.

Jane walked us proudly to the row of stretch limousines that awaited us and as we entered the first I could see Sarah flinch. She hated overstatement, particularly with automobiles, and on top of that, part of our visit was for charity purposes. 'This will never do,' she began, and launched into Jane. 'All I need is for the press to say "Freebie Fergie Takes Limo to Visit Orphans".'

She was right, of course – that is exactly what would have been written.

To make matters worse, the chief of security sat in the passenger seat and felt that he ought to make conversation with the angry Duchess. This fellow spoke almost exactly like the New York detective who interviewed me along with Scotland Yard. In a thick Brooklyn accent, he commented that New York was pretty covered with snow. 'Except that it's yellow snow by now!' he added with a laugh.

By the time we had arrived at the hotel Sarah had dressed down Jane and Christine and ensured that less ostentatious vehicles should be found. I had to agree. Such cars might be suitable for over-compensating real estate tycoons and their vulgar wives, but were not exactly the right image for a member of the British royal family. Jane took the criticism with more anger than I had noticed before. An interesting pattern emerged which would become increasingly clear throughout the trip, and subsequent visits to the States. Lady Jane resented being treated like a servant outside the UK, and particularly in America. I think that Jane believed the differences in British social status and accent were not so apparent to Americans, who were just pleased to meet guests somehow associated with the royal family. Consequently, Lady Jane was at her most ladylike when sipping a drink in the famous lounge of The Carlisle or strolling through Bloomingdales by the side of the Duchess.

The Duchess's suite at The Carlisle was sumptuous. It was elegantly decorated with Old Master paintings, and featured a grand piano in the sitting-room. In actuality, it was owned by a partner of Bill Simon and was his pied-à-terre, not simply a generic New York hotel room. I was initially given the room next to the Duchess, with a connecting door between the rooms, but we were afraid of rumours so I switched with Jane and took a room around the corridor. We prepared for a gruelling five-day schedule which would take us from meetings with television executives to drug rehabilitation centres, halfway houses for HIV-positive children, and would include a score of television and newspaper interviews.

On the first night we all met at the lounge for drinks and I noticed that Lady Jane and Christine were dressed to the nines. The Duchess and I exchanged glances and then Sarah said, 'Aren't we posh tonight?' Jane blushed and looked at Christine, who turned an even deeper shade of crimson. 'Well, ma'am,' explained Christine, 'I met someone the other night who is quite nice . . .'

'I see,' murmured the understanding Duchess. 'And you, Jane?'

'I have plans too, ma'am,' was all she would tell us.

Christine had a way of falling in love rather quickly. At one point she had met a Guards officer at a party and told me the next day that she was about to be engaged. This trip provided Christine with the opportunity to again fall quickly in love – and it seemed she had already done so. I was not at all surprised by her behaviour, but I sensed that something covert was going on with Jane. She looked far too pleased with herself, and far too happy about her mysterious appearance. As the days passed it seemed that both ladies had discovered a thriving social life in New York which began precisely when their mistress was finished with them for the night.

Sarah and I began the first full day with a breakfast meeting in a conference room full of hard-nosed television and marketing executives. We were trying to sell the US television rights for Budgie, and also to develop all the associated merchandising. Despite our exhausting trip to Bosnia and the previous day of travelling, Sarah was magnificent. She spontaneously spun out several fantastic Budgie inventions, to include a Budgie pram which was pulled, not pushed, so that the parent would be forced to cross a street ahead of their child. After the meeting we had back-to-back television interviews, and naturally we brought Lady Jane in her more menial capacity as dresser. Between the interviews we had only a few minutes and when I entered the changing-room I was amazed to see Jane blow-drying Sarah's armpits; the harsh studio lighting had made the Duchess perspire through her blouse. I might not have found this scene amusing a year before, but now Lady Jane seemed far too grand to be holding a hairdryer over the armpit of another person – even a royal duchess.

Shortly after this somewhat demeaning duty, Lady Jane was offered the chance to become etiquette mentor to another aspiring socialite. Sonya, the attractive female security guard, had been studying the royal protocol with growing interest. Finally, she approached me to ask, 'What is that thing that Jane keeps on doing?' Before I could make the sarcastic remark I had intended, the young lady leaned forward and bent her knees as if she were doing some sort of aerobic exercise. I realised that she was trying to curtsey. I immediately requested the presence of Lady Jane, who demonstrated the proper way to execute a curtsey. After a few minutes of practice Sonya thanked her, saying: 'We all like the Duchess, and want to do the right thing.' The next time Sonya saw the Duchess, we were in a large room filled with advertising executives. The young lady cried: 'Yo, Your Royal Highness, check this out!' and executed a perfect curtsey, despite the considerable weight of all her firearms.

That afternoon we had lunch arrangements with Bill Simon at the famous Le Cirque restaurant. After the interviews were finished we were driven to this watering hole of the élite, or, to be more correct, the last generation of élite. For in actuality Le Cirque, like Bill Simon, had reached its peak in the mid-'70s. It has subsequently gone through a rebirth, but in 1994 it served as a sort of Madame Tussaud's for the waxwork figures who had had their heyday in the '70s. Bill said to us, 'The hardest thing in the world is going from Who's Who to "who's that",' and I think that most of the diners at Le

Cirque that day would not have disagreed. Each table seemed adorned with an aged version of a once-familiar face. Barbara Walters sat across from us, celebrating the birthday of *Cosmopolitan*'s Helen Gurley-Brown, and both ladies nodded politely as we sat down. They discreetly ignored us until they were about to leave, at which point each lady greeted the Duchess and invited her to an interview any time she chose.

Princess Elizabeth of Yugoslavia was also in attendance. Elizabeth had been hailed as the great beauty of the jet set throughout the '60s. Her daughter is one of the stars of *Dynasty* and shares the exquisite beauty of her mother. A well-known writer sat at an adjacent booth, staring at Bill. 'She is quite famous,' he said knowingly. 'She writes all kinds of sex stories – autobiographical, I think . . .' added Bill, as he glanced over at the mummified face wearing the make-up and hairstyle of its youth.

An attractive woman with two less attractive friends came over for a moment to offer the Duchess a copy of the book they had just released on the significance of engagement rings. They looked longingly at the Duchess's ruby, and the attractive author exclaimed: 'Rubies are a stone of passion – he must love you very much.' Being that Sarah's marriage was not a state secret, I felt that this was a very obvious ploy. Next came the inevitable question, 'Could I photograph it for my next book? It has a great deal of psychological significance.' Sarah wisely refused permission, and the ladies reluctantly left us to continue our lunch. Next, the maître d' came over to pay his inevitable respects. 'What a lovely tie you have,' remarked the polite Duchess. The fellow returned a few minutes later with his tie neatly wrapped in a box.

Lady Jane and Christine had seated themselves at the bar, as Bill had not invited them to join us for lunch. Although I was enjoying trying to identify the people in the room, and despite the fascinating conversation we were having at our own table, I was transfixed by the activity at the bar. Lady Jane had made it clear that she was 'with' the Duchess. As a result, people either too frightened or too polite to accost us directly had made a pilgrimage to Jane. It began with an overdressed fellow who was chatting up Jane with incredible enthusiasm, in a strong Oxford accent. He seemed a little effete and would periodically dab at his nose with a large, red silk handkerchief. Nevertheless, he convinced Jane to escort him to our table where he introduced himself, whipped out a number of business cards with an impressive crest engraved upon them, indicating that he was a knight, and then simply sat down next to us. Sarah glared at Lady Jane, who retreated to the now overflowing bar where she continued to hold court.

As it turns out, the knight's only association with any queen was the fact that he had been born in Queens. His accent, like his title, had been purchased. He was a knight of some tiny principality whose only export products were mineral water and titles. Bill finally asked this pest to leave.

A few minutes later Lady Jane approached the table, a little more tentatively than she had the last time; in fact, she had brought Christine for reinforcement. Sarah glared at the two ladies suspiciously. 'Well?' she asked crisply.

'Your Royal Highness,' began Lady Jane – always reverting to strictest protocol while under siege – 'there is a large party in the next room for Princess Elizabeth's Foundation and Princess Elizabeth sends her regards and reminds you that she is related to His Royal Highness, and wonders if she might pay her respects to you now.'

This was a diplomatic speech if ever I heard one. I wondered if Jane had formulated that manipulative message. It was polite, reminded one of family ties and was virtually impossible to refuse.

'In a few minutes,' capitulated Sarah, looking apologetically at Bill.

'I certainly don't mind,' replied the billionaire, happy to be once again the centre of attention. 'Ah, yes,' he sighed. 'This place has always been a beehive of activity; Nixon loved it so much he would have them cater the White House dinners – they would fly in the food in planefuls.'

So Princess Elizabeth was escorted over with an entourage of charity volunteers. She was even more beautiful than I had expected, with long black hair and big blue eyes. I stood up to greet her and she stared at me for a little longer than was usual. 'Have we met before?' she asked. 'It feels as if we have . . .' I replied. Sarah and Elizabeth made conversation and agreed that members of the board of Elizabeth's Foundation would contact me regarding joint efforts in Yugoslavia. But as Elizabeth left, she offered me her private phone number and asked how long I would be staying in New York.

After lunch we had decided to go shopping in Bloomingdales, so we said goodbye to Bill and mounted our cavalcade of (now smaller) black cars. Sarah, Lady Jane and I sat together in the back.

'Flirting, were we, little Starkie?' asked the Duchess.

'I hoped she was flirting with me,' I responded.

'Then call her – ask her for a date,' said a taunting Duchess as she handed me her mobile phone.

'Fine,' I answered, taking the bait, and called immediately. Elizabeth seemed to be expecting the call and agreed to dinner the following night. Jane and Sarah both glared at me as if I had cheated on them individually.

'So, Starkie, one Royal Highness is no longer enough. First it was Princess Esmeralda and now her – aren't we the little social climber!'

'How can you say that?' I exploded. 'I called her because she is beautiful, Esmeralda is just a friend, and my current girlfriend is a secretary – and I almost dated Jane, for heaven's sake!'

I had not meant to say that, of course. I was just angry, but it was like shoving a stake in Jane's heart. She turned white, lowered her eyes and would not say a word. Of course I apologised, but it was too late.

We arrived at the side entrance of Bloomingdales, where we were met by a personal shopper named Ivy, whom the Duchess had already used in the past. Sarah walked next to Ivy, with Jane on her other side. I followed behind with the growing contingent of sales people required to carry the ever-increasing pile of clothing. We progressed from designer label to designer label with Ivy stopping periodically to show off an article of which she was particularly proud, always using the words, 'It's new, it's fun . . . it's you!' Our cargo-bearers were barely able to keep up with us when we finally reached the relative safety of the dressing-rooms. I sat down and waited as Lady Jane and Sarah disappeared into a changing-room. It was a small room completely panelled with mirrors, and had a large curtain for a door. Jane was still not talking to me, but Sarah insisted that I give the 'thumbs up, or down' for every outfit.

It was nearing closing time, and since it was Valentine's Day our attendants were getting anxious. We had a few minutes to proceed to the children's department where Sarah simply pointed to anything she liked and said, 'In four and six,' as the attendants scrambled through the racks.

On the way out we looked into a case of antique jewellery, where

Sarah found an old pocket-watch for John. She looked longingly at a simple silver necklace that she seemed to love, but walked away sadly when she saw the price. John had given her a strange gift that year for Valentine's Day. It was a small ring which resembled a wedding ring – a pathetic reminder of his impatience. So I told Sarah that I would meet her back in the hotel, and bought the necklace for her. Tracking down Jane when I got back to The Carlisle, I again apologised, saying, ' I really did not mean to imply that you were less important because you are not a princess. I meant that you were all equal.' Lady Jane looked somewhat sceptical at this explanation, so I continued with: 'Could you do me a favour?' Instead of the exuberant support that such a request had once elicited, I received an uninterested look and the question of, 'Hum, well, what is it then?'

'I bought that necklace that she liked for the Duchess, and want to put it under her pillow, like we once did with the icon. Can I go through your room?'

'I suppose so,' replied the put-out lady.

Naturally, I pretended that the gift was from John and even wrote a note with a string of obligatory, childish endearments typical of him. It seemed to please her, and years later John would use the incident as an example of his attentiveness – forgetting that he was barely informed of it.

That night an interesting development occurred. Sarah realised that John Kennedy was in town and this sent her into a frenzy. She came to my room more excited than I had seen her in years. 'Starkie, *HE* is *HERE*!' she exclaimed.

'Who?' was my tired response.

'John Kennedy, and I am convinced that we would be perfect for each other. I had Jane and Christine track him down and we have a meeting set for tomorrow night.'

I came close to either suggesting that we double date, or accusing *her* of being the social climber; instead I simply pointed out, 'You know he is dating Daryl Hannah?'

'So?' was her indignant reply.

As it turned out, we were both to be disappointed.

The next morning, prior to a visit to a drug rehabilitation centre, I received a message from Princess Elizabeth's office saying that she had to cancel our dinner due to another engagement. I was surprised that she had not even called me herself and went to ask Sarah for her advice, reading her the terse message I had received.

'She had her secretary call?' she asked with astonishment.

'Yes, it doesn't look too good, does it?' I replied sadly.

And then Sarah did something I will never forget. People who know the strange dynamics of our relationship often ask, 'Why did you stay with her for so long?' What she did next was part of the answer. As it turned out, the Duchess had made plans to have lunch with Elizabeth that day. Without a pause she picked up the telephone and dialled Elizabeth's number. A secretary answered and Sarah did not even bother to ask for the Princess. She simply said: 'This is the Duchess of York; would you please tell Princess Elizabeth that I must cancel our lunch meeting as I have another engagement.' As she placed the receiver down she looked at me with those twinkling eyes that expressed so much, and said simply: 'If my Starkie isn't good enough for her, then she is not good enough for me.' A few minutes later Lady Jane came in through the connecting doors to inform us that John Kennedy had to cancel their meeting as he had a pressing appointment. I only wish that I could have reciprocated, but I doubt if my message would have meant anything to him at all. Sarah took it well, saying, 'I bet Daryl found out about the meeting and made him cancel it, the jealous cow!'

So Sarah and I found ourselves without dates that evening and decided that we would use the time to meet Christine's new boyfriend. She told us she would be seeing him at a particular bar not too far from our hotel. During the course of that day, Sarah had been forced to scold Christine. At one point we were told that the Duchess would be meeting 'a couple of doctors' at the Cornell Medical Center. When we arrived Sarah was put in front of a podium and expected to address a full house of medical professionals. When we located Christine to ask why we had not been informed, we found her closeted in a coatroom chatting away with her new boyfriend. Sarah took her aside and let loose. I guess she was eager to meet the person that had so distracted her assistant.

It was a crisp winter night and New York was still digging itself out of huge snowdrifts. The sky was clear and we could even see a few stars, so we walked to the nearby bar. Christine was seated at a table with perhaps four other people, all male. They were all ex-pat Brits and South Africans, yet not one of the men rose when the

Duchess approached. We sat down on the hard, wooden chairs and I commented on how uncomfortable they were. Christine's new boyfriend responded: 'Imagine how hard they are for Christine after the bollocking she received today.' We were aghast. This fellow was a stranger to the Duchess, yet he was apprised of something of what had transpired that day. He went on to ask if the Duchess was looking forward to her upcoming trip to Closters – something of which the press was not yet informed. We did not even bother to accept a drink, returning instead to the safety of The Carlisle to listen to Eartha Kitt singing in the lounge.

Again Jane was nowhere to be seen. She too had found someone, but his identity was to remain a secret. But the night-stalking Jane would soon meet a substantial quarry. Here in New York she was still discreet, but her caution and her patience were waning. Soon the rumours that had begun would have names and places associated with them. But for now, Lady Jane was simply missing in action.

The week in New York finally ended and Christine asked permission to remain for another few days with her boyfriend. I had work to do in New York and so Sarah and Lady Jane returned to London together. Sarah was so pleased that the trip had cost very little that she flew back on Concorde, accompanied by the now supersonic girl from Grimsby.

In recognition of Lady Jane's new status, she was to be given her own company car and selected a Fiesta with as many options as could be managed. It was all ever so corporate. Prior to this, Jane had suffered an injury while driving one of Sarah's rented Fords; while turning into Wentworth Drive, not far from the gates of Romenda, she was hit in the rear by another car. She managed to drive the damaged Ford back to the house, where she showed the wreckage to the butler Tony Blackmore. She assured him that she had not been badly injured and the car was exchanged. The next time I visited the Duchess I was shocked to see Jane trussed in a formidable neck-brace. 'I had no idea you were so badly hurt!' I exclaimed with genuine concern. She smiled weakly at me and closed her eyes for a moment, as if she needed to muster the strength to discuss her martyrdom. I have no way of knowing how serious her injuries really were but she managed to avoid the duties which involved carrying even moderately heavy objects. In fact, she often recruited the aid of the palace's Chamber Floor footmen to help her load packages into the car.

As the year progressed, Sarah had developed a strong business and even pseudo-social relationship with a charming Cockney businessman named Clive Garrad. He reminded me of one of those streetwise street urchins from Dickens's novel *Oliver Twist*, and he was constantly coming up with new schemes to make money. He assisted us in the purchase of a very expensive horse for the Duchess and she was grateful. Among his creative schemes Clive came to the conclusion that the property value of any home in which the Duchess lived would appreciate substantially. As a result, he offered to contribute to the rental cost of a villa in the South of France for Sarah's use that summer. The idea was that Clive would purchase the villa and resell it for a large profit. It was a good idea, and I suggested that Sarah paint a mural on the foyer wall to *really* impress a potential buyer. Sarah was taking painting lessons at the time, and I thought that even a fairly well-executed mural would be just the thing to prove that this was once a 'royal dwelling'.

Sarah asked me to help her locate a suitable property, but I did not have the time, so Lady Jane was recruited to explore the rental market in the area around Cannes. This reconnaissance trip would foreshadow a number of pivotal events in Jane's life. It would further familiarise her with this elegant region, and facilitate her future travels to the South of France with Cressman. Additionally, it set the precedent that among Lady Jane's growing duties would now be included the task of selecting Sarah's summer homes. Oddly, it would be this task that would be instrumental in the loss of her job.

Lady Jane returned from her mission with an impressive number of photos of prospective homes, and ultimately Sarah chose a beautiful Mediterranean-style villa called Maison de la Fontaine, five miles from Cannes. The home was ideal with the exception that it lacked separate servants' quarters, and so a small house was rented several miles away to house the staff. Lady Jane assisted in readying the home and at the Duchess's request prepared baskets in each guest-room filled with condoms and lubricants, just as many hotels offer baskets of fruit.

Sarah invited her friend Pamela Stephenson, the wife of comedian Billy Connolly, to the villa and a number of friends came to stay over for periods of time. Oddly, the Amblers were invited as guests and, instead of staying at the staff house, were offered accommodation in the villa. To make matters more confusing, at one point they shared their meals with the Duchess, yet later the butler was castigated for not setting a separate table for them. Although the Duchess did not want them to eat with the servants, she did not want them to share all their meals with her either. It would have meant creating three separate settings, to really underscore the uncertain social hierarchy. On the other hand, the Duchess made it painfully clear that she felt no such compunctions when it came to Lady Jane. During the periods when Jane was present she was clearly treated like the other servants, not a personal guest. Nevertheless, she enjoyed sunbathing with Sarah and amazed the staff by her decision to spend large portions of the day topless. This seemed to cause her husband some degree of embarrassment.

At the same time John Bryan and I had decided to spend our summer vacation in Sardinia. John had recently been selected by the French and Italian fashion syndicate as one of the best-dressed men in the world. The president of this organisation was a dashing and charming Italian playboy named Massimo Gargia, with an illustrious pedigree of famous conquests which even included Garbo. John and I had been spending a lot of time in this new social scene and elected to spend the summer with our new group of friends.

John was furious at not being invited to spend the summer with Sarah, and decided to take his revenge in the way he felt most comfortable. In this case it was to bed a gorgeous French princess, and even to tolerate the new relationship being photographed and published with the caption 'A Princess on Both Sides Instead of a Duchess by Marriage'. Although Sarah had hoped that John would not resort to such extreme measures, she nevertheless commissioned Lady Jane to create a bundle of summer shirts featuring John's home phone number embroidered on the pocket, where initials would usually be found. 'It will make it easier to chat up girls and save lots of time,' she teased, not really expecting that he would take it so literally. In retaliation Sarah allowed herself to be photographed swimming next to the handsome son of James Mason. Lady Jane would often witness this type of harmless flirting and somehow seemed to believe that it went further than it really did – for in emulating Sarah's flirtatiousness, Jane simply was unable or unwilling to draw a line before it went too far. The summer ended with a lot of hard feelings. Sarah's staff was upset by the confusing social hierarchy, Sarah was livid with John and me, while John was angry at Sarah's flirtatiousness. The only person to come out of August unscathed was Lady Jane.

CHAPTER ELEVEN

GETTING A PENGUIN

FOR ALMOST THE NEXT two years Jane would consolidate then expand her role and influence within the rarified world of Sarah's inner circle. To explain how she accomplished this it is first necessary to understand how the dynamics of the group worked. The Court of Fergie was a somewhat chaotic place, but in a sense it probably resembled or mimicked many royal courts. The objective was survival and control; and often control would simply devolve upon those able to survive the longest. Garnering power was a zero-sum game. There was only so much influence Sarah was willing to accept, and an army of people competing to offer it. As 1994 progressed, Sarah became enamoured with a host of fresh individuals vying for her attentions. Although she never consciously implemented my plan of dividing her life into three functional categories, somehow events and these new personalities channelled her that way.

She rediscovered her love of horses, and found an instructor and confidant in Cork, Ireland. Sarah and I would travel there almost weekly, but it was always with Jane Ambler, not with Lady Jane. Sarah's personal and equestrian lives were the territory of Jane Ambler, who became a de facto social secretary. Not only did she orchestrate trips and social functions, she often attended these events as a guest. It would be the Amblers, not the Dunn-Butlers, who would be included on the microscopic guest list of Sarah's birthday party that October, for example.

The charity front was dominated by a woman named Deborah Oxley. Although deemed unqualified to fill the role of secretary to

John Bryan, she was able to oust the dedicated co-founder of Children in Crisis who, despite capability and sincerity, lacked the required degree of political cunning to survive. For a short period Deborah's dominance was challenged by my establishment of a German children's foundation with the Duchess, but she managed to weather that threat.

As a result, the only room that really existed to create a niche of control was within Sarah's business life, for John Bryan was finally being phased out. It would take until the summer of 1995 and the threat of an international arrest warrant before the break would be complete, but each month saw John's influence dwindle further. Sarah searched for someone to fill that void and a talent contest began. Soon, retired generals, cockney businessmen, Saudi princes and even oriental consortiums were tried and then discarded. At one point Sarah and I even inaugurated an operational company together, which we called Fireside Communications. John, sensing his imminent redundancy, did his best to sabotage the effort and I withdrew to keep the peace. Sarah was naturally aware of these contests for power and even seemed to enjoy watching them. She called me once to say, 'My therapist advised me to stand still and let them all dance around me until they exhaust themselves – slowly, slowly catchee monkey.'

Lady Jane never really danced – she never expended much energy at all. She waited us all out, and in the end she would be one of the last survivors. Her husband gave up his struggle early on and left the service of the Duchess. The casualties mounted quickly, and each loss further reinforced Jane's seniority.

Tony Blackmore, the Buckingham Palace-trained butler, simply exploded with rage one day. He returned from the summer in the South of France very upset by the social chaos which had been precipitated by the polarised treatment afforded to the two Janes. The summer activities at the rented house disturbed Tony's precise expectations of royal protocol. He objected to the disparity in treatment of the two Janes in relation to their housing and dining arrangements, and found the social turmoil to be confusing and disruptive to the staff. Based on his impressive record as footman to Her Majesty, and his loyal service to the Yorks, the Duchess offered him 24 hours to apologise. He would not. Tony was one of the few employees to retain his dignity. The Duchess knew she could count on him to offer her sound advice. His loss was a great blow, for it left Sarah more isolated. Sally Hughes, the attentive and respected nanny, quit suddenly, citing her desire to become a kindergarten schoolteacher, despite her consuming love for Beatrice and Eugenie. She left the staff, resulting in another painful transition. In the four years that I knew Sarah well she was forced to change nannies three times. As a result Lady Jane was probably the most constant female companion for the little princesses, whom she had known all their lives.

Yeltsin, the now semi-Anglicised guide, returned to the Himalayas. Never really able to master the English language, we had to admit that his duties on the telephone were somewhat disappointing. We had next tried to qualify him for a driving licence – and succeeded in terrifying the driving instructor, as well as our own driver, with Yeltsin's difficulties behind the wheel. The final try at educating our Sherpa guide was the futile but very humorous attempt by Christopher Dunn-Butler to teach Yeltsin how to use a computer. Sadly, all these efforts might have created great stories, but ultimately failed to westernise Yeltsin. He left with a full heart and good memories. We can only assume that he carried the image of his 'god' to a suitable shrine on the face of mighty Everest.

Terence Wilson-Fletcher, the back-up cook, simply backed out one day and decided to devote his time to painting portraits. Like so many members of staff he developed a romantic relationship with one of his colleagues and a love-hate relationship with his boss. Even Sarah's newly minted PA, Christine Gallagher, requested to be transferred to New York, where she could involve herself with business and charity activities using the Atlantic Ocean as a buffer from her mistress's court.

A plague had hit the Court of Fergie – fever raged, tempers were high and the stricken fell. At the end of the day, only two real survivors were left on the field: Jane Ambler and Lady Jane.

During this process Lady Jane continued her strange metamorphosis and the change was now not simply restricted to her personality. Jane began to change physically; her hair colour mysteriously migrated towards shades of red. The inevitable Alice in Wonderland band that she had worn like a slave collar was nowhere to be seen, and her fiery new mane flew freely in the breeze. Her wardrobe began to resemble that of her mistress and her gestures and language became more flamboyant. In a word, Lady Jane became Fergie-esque. It became so extreme that at times the press was confused about which one was the Duchess.

Despite the feigned physical similarities, the problem remained that Lady Jane could not really duplicate Sarah's charm. It was as if the Duchess had been squeezed under the lid of a Xerox machine and someone had pressed 'copy' — what came out was a black-and-white, somewhat distorted version of a vibrantly colourful original which defied duplication. The essence of the Duchess was not contained in a jar of hair colour, nor in any particular combination of clothing. Jane was destined to fail.

In compensation for this failure Lady Jane became rather promiscuous. Erroneously imagining that the key to Sarah's charm lay in sex, Jane exaggerated that aspect of her as well. By the end of 1994, members of Sarah's staff were trying to keep track of Jane's conquests. With each visit, increasingly alarmed members of the Duchess's staff would inform me of Jane's newest adventures. Her exploits would include an affair with a noted member of the press.

Her relationship with the journalist would begin in the unlikely locale of Kenya. Sarah had taken Lady Jane on a strange visit to Africa, during which the pair were surrounded by journalists. At this point Jane was assisting me with a project to control media coverage. We essentially isolated the Duchess from the baying photographers and would plan photo opportunities with a chosen journalist and crew. We had selected the daughter of the King of Belgium, Princess Esmeralda, as the designated reporter. On the Kenyan trip Sarah would call me at a particular time to announce, 'I will unlock the door to my suite in ten minutes.' I would then call Esmeralda and her Tunisian fiancé and they would have a photographer open the door at the designated time and snap the valuable photo.

Lady Jane was assisting me with these complex orchestrations, and in the case of the Kenyan trip seems to have confused her priorities, for instead of assisting our journalist, she fell in love with another one. Edward Verity was employed by the *Daily Mail*. In the tabloid wars in which Diana fought Charles and Sarah competed with Diana, the *Mail* had been the major field of battle. The readers of the *Mail* were exactly the type of people that the royals wished to address; consequently, *Mail* journalists were relatively well treated and would often befriend a particular member of the royal family. Richard Kay, for example, became such a close friend of the Princess of Wales that he remained silent about issues that might have earned him an enormous fortune.

Lady Jane was aware of the respect afforded to the *Mail*. Soon she would have her own *Mail* confidant. The two would remain on friendly terms for the next four years – and then the relationship would turn romantic and very sexual. It is interesting in hindsight to read Verity's expansive feature story on Jane from December 1995, in which he writes about her with obvious admiration, even describing her as 'willowy'. That is how she had appeared to me in the role she played during the bar scene at Cap Ferrat, when she gave me the *Wuthering Heights* book. Apparently, her reprisal of this role was just as convincing and lasted considerably longer.

But these successes did not offer the complete social legitimacy that Lady Jane craved. As she consolidated her position within Sarah's court, she longed to find a consort suitable to her great expectations. That goal seemed within reach on one elegant evening in the late spring of 1995.

Our charity galas had become quite prestigious by this time. We held them in venues such as the Royal Guildhall and they were invariably formal, well planned, and well attended. They would generally begin with a dinner, where the guests sat at tables of about ten people. After the obligatory speeches and slide shows, the event would end with an auction to raise money for the upcoming project. In the case of this event, we were in the process of building a recuperative home for Polish children recovering from leukaemia. The region around the city of Krakow was so polluted that an inordinate number of children contracted the disease. Even if they received successful treatment, they would often relapse upon return to their homes. We decided to build a children's home in the cleaner environment of the adjacent mountains. Graf (Count) von Krakow was a personal friend and I had introduced him to Sarah. The reunified German government had recently returned his family's enormous estates, some of which were in Poland. Von Krakow kindly offered to donate a castle or hunting lodge to our project, but somehow Children in Crisis seemed unable to coordinate the donation and we were forced to raise money for another building.

The auctions were often very lucrative and on this spring evening

in London we hoped to raise a large sum. There is a sense of
competition among the bidders at such events and I had seen some
very astonishing examples of generous bidding in the past. The
former head of Children in Crisis had painted a Christmas scene
which was heralded as the major item for a previous auction. Sadly,
when the bidding began, nobody seemed willing to make even the
smallest offer. There was an embarrassed silence for a few seconds;
Richard Branson, the great British entrepreneur and supporter of our
charity, then suddenly sprang to his feet and, running to the
podium, snatched the painting from the hands of the astonished
auctioneer, announcing: 'I bid four thousand for this and nobody
had better outbid me, because I must have it.'

Such events require a huge number of organisers and assistants,
and Sarah would mobilise a regiment of attractive young women to
help. Her personal staff was invariably present, and after assisting
with the preparations were permitted to take their seats among the
other guests. Lady Jane had put a great effort into looking her
aristocratic best that night; yet I noticed that she seemed distracted.
Perhaps she was already aware of a particular name on the guest list
– or maybe she just reckoned that such an event was a potential
goldmine for a prospective gold-digger. There was, after all,
precedent to be hopeful. As Jane was aware, Christine had bagged a
polo player at such an event, just one year prior. I recalled the
episode well. I found Christine rearranging the seating cards on my
table. When she realised I had caught her, she exclaimed, 'Allan, if I
don't sit near you I will die!' In actuality Christine had no interest in
my company but had already fixed her sights on an attractive polo
player named Michael, who was seated across from me. They began
a fairly long-term relationship that evening, so it was not without
hope that Lady Jane now flitted about the Hall, smiling her best
Sarah smile, and lowering her chin in the most seductively Sarah
way. And it was on that very evening that Lady Jane was destined to
outdo her wildest expectations. It was here that she was to win a
real-life Greek shipping tycoon. Had not the widow of the beloved
President Kennedy, iconised mother of the coveted John-John, not
wed a Greek shipping tycoon? Was there not an undeniable cachet
associated with these Mediterranean merchants, only matched by
the suave sophistication of a South American polo player? Clearly
Dimitri Horne, son of the socially prominent Lemos family, had been

placed by fate in that party so that Lady Jane might finally be offered the glass slipper which would make her transformation complete. Greece, after all, is a long way from Grimsby.

Jane fell in love. I sensed the attraction that night, even suspecting that they might already know each other. I heard later from the other members of staff that Jane had actually met Dimitri some time earlier on an aeroplane – and that seemed much more likely. It would be a number of weeks before Jane would actually confess her relationship to me, and that would be under rather strange circumstances.

I must say that Dimitri is a very elegant fellow. He was somewhat taller than Jane, rather dapper, well spoken, and he actually worked. Despite his privileged birth he seemed to take his professional life very seriously. Dimitri had a flat in Kensington and very shortly after this meeting the two would become a couple, with an active social life. But before our Peloponnesian prince would add his stamp of legitimacy to Lady Jane's social credentials, I would have my final and most memorable encounter with her.

It happened in Poland.

Jane and I had last been in Poland in November 1992. It had been the very first Eastern European trip for Sarah's new charity. On that trip, a Jane who now no longer existed had been so in love with me that I had had to cut my trip short rather than face her jealousy. This time things were very different.

We began the trip in Warsaw. Sarah had invited an associate of Bill Simon to join us. Peter Bougdanos (another wealthy Greek, who even resembled Dimitri) ran Simon's merger and acquisition operation in Europe. He was one of my closest friends and had been informed about my strange relationship with Jane. Since that memorable lunch at Le Cirque, Sarah had maintained a close link with the wealthy Simon, and now she hoped to convince Peter to donate a swimming-pool to the new children's home.

The previous December the Duchess and I had co-founded a German children's charity called MIN. My intent was that Peter should make his donation through this organisation. During a long train trip from Warsaw to Krakow, Sarah sequestered herself in a private compartment with members of the board of Children in Crisis. I was not invited and she even seemed to be avoiding direct eye contact with me. After so many years I was aware of the pathology of this type of behaviour and immediately sought out Jane. She seemed reluctant to speak to me and I simply could not get her alone on the train.

Upon arrival in Krakow we were driven in a minibus to the mountain retreat. It was the official opening of the home and there were a lot of official duties for the Duchess to perform. As the festivities became less formal and a Polish folk band began to play, I again tried to find Jane. She was standing behind the Duchess, in almost precisely the same pose as her mistress, almost like an understudy preparing her lines in the hope that she will one day get to perform herself. I motioned to her and she seemed to see, but ignored me. I stood there, exasperated, waiting by the minibus. Next to me stood the driver. He was a tall, gaunt, fair-haired fellow in his late twenties.

'Fancy her?' he asked with annoying over-familiarity, as he broke into a smile revealing a number of missing teeth.

'Excuse me?' I asked.

'Jane,' he said, actually pointing at her. 'Do you fancy her?'

'We are old friends,' I finally said, avoiding the impulse to smack him for his impudence. Jane's reputation had deteriorated considerably, but I was not willing to accept open contempt for her morality.

'I had her last night,' he went on, as if we were two old mates in a pub.

'What?' I exploded, furious at this insinuation.

Mistaking my outburst for interest and approval, he continued, 'Yeah, I fucked her last night, and let me tell you she is dirty!'

Well, to be honest I was a little intrigued by this. I did not understand what he meant by 'dirty', so I reluctantly asked, 'What is that supposed to mean?'

'I mean she does everything and likes it rough,' explained the rogue. 'I mean that she enjoys being knocked about a little,' he continued with a laugh.

I found this fellow repulsive – but I must admit that I actually believed him. It was a very similar reaction to the one I had when I received the call from Scotland Yard. At first one feels great surprise then, on reflection, well, it seems possible. This toothless fellow was bursting with such obvious pride in what he must have considered to be a posh conquest that he was very convincing.

At last Lady Jane approached the minibus and I will be damned if the two of them did not smile knowingly at one another. She looked over at me and offered a tentative smile, as if she had time for a few quick words.

'Jane,' I began, 'I know that the Duchess was meeting with her . . .' But before I could finish, she said quickly, 'I really cannot discuss it now, Allan, I am very busy,' denying me an audience. 'Maybe later,' she offered graciously; *noblesse oblige*, you know.

We returned to the hotel in Krakow and prepared for a black-tie dinner event. Peter and I had to share the same hotel room. As we dressed for dinner we recapped the events of our trip thus far. 'Do they really expect me to write out a cheque for a swimming-pool when the Duchess has not even said ten words to me?' asked Peter.

'Yes,' I sighed.

Sarah's behaviour at dinner was terrifying. She oozed goodwill suspiciously towards me and placed me next to her at the table. The seating arrangement was odd, in that the Duchess was seated in the centre of a long table, not at the head. It was a bit like the scene from the Last Supper, with me to her left. She used her menu as a screen and whispered to me for much of the meal, demanding at one point: 'Starkie, please fuck the spy tonight and tell me what the hell she is up to.' She was referring to an attractive lady from the embassy whom we believed was reporting Sarah's activities to the Foreign Office.

'I don't think she has too much to report, but why have you been avoiding me?'

'Insecure, are we? Don't be silly, of course I am not avoiding you – well, we have a breakfast meeting tomorrow before we leave . . . bring Peter.'

That sounded ominous, but I supposed it could just be a team-effort to squeeze a large donation out of him.

Lady Jane was at the far end of the great table and I must say she looked very good. She was wearing a black dress which clung tightly to her, with a gaping slit up one side. Around her neck she had some sort of a choker. Her hair was blown out and it fell in a wave over the side of her face. But the clinical manner in which she regarded my interaction with the Duchess filled me with a suspicion that she was studying the way Sarah conducted a difficult operation. I knew that it was imperative to get Jane alone that night and find out what she knew.

As dinner was finishing, Sarah launched into her usual four favourite jokes. As she finished the second, she glanced over at me and asked, 'Would it shock the spy if I told the penguin joke?' I thought it would be good fun to shock the staid diplomats, for the joke was rather vulgar. I will briefly summarise it, for it was to play a small role in the later events of the evening.

The joke is about a sailor on shore leave who, despite only possessing £10, solicits a prostitute. He asks what is available and is told that full sex is £30 while oral sex is only £20. When he explains that he only has £10, the prostitute offers to perform a penguin. Unsure of what this means, but eager to achieve some form of release, he agrees. The prostitute proceeds to go to her knees (the Duchess would actually mime this), then unzips his trousers (Sarah would make an unzipping motion) and then begins to perform oral sex on him. As the pleasantly surprised sailor announces that he is close to ejaculation, the prostitute (beautifully acted out by the Duchess) would simply stand up and walk away. The interrupted sailor, with trousers around his knees and hands extended comically to his side (now reversing her role, the Duchess also portrayed this) would hobble towards the prostitute – walking exactly like a penguin.

As Sarah began the joke, we were interrupted by a shrill, wailing sound. This unnerved the gifted Duchess, disturbing her joke. 'What on earth is that?' she asked.

'An old Krakow tradition,' explained the diplomat. 'It has gone on for centuries, since the city was saved by a lone bugler on its walls.'

'Let's have a look,' cried the now excited Sarah. And like a group of schoolchildren we ran together towards the eerie music.

Krakow, like Prague, has a large section of the original stone city wall still intact. On a turret over the main gateway we could see the silhouette of a man holding a trumpet. As we stood there in the darkness, the melody suddenly ended as the bugler played a last, drawn-out wailing note, which died abruptly. Centuries ago his predecessor had been shot with an arrow from an archer of the invading army; yet his warning had awakened the garrison and the city was saved. It was almost identical to Kipling's story of Gunga

Din. We were all moved.

As the echo of the last wailing note faded I spotted Jane standing in the shadow of the barbican. Approaching her I asked, 'Can we speak alone now?' Perhaps it was the strange effect of the music or maybe some part of the old Jane still existed, but she looked at me as if she were lost in a dream. 'Yes, of course we can,' said the familiar voice of an old friend I had not seen in a while. We walked back to the bar of the hotel, and it was mobbed with the majority of the guests from dinner. Peter looked over at me and I noticed that he was busy entertaining two attractive ladies. Jane eyed her watch nervously and I wondered if she had a rendezvous scheduled with the driver. 'It is too crowded here,' I said. 'Let's go up to my room for a minute.' I truly meant this innocently – it would have been impossible not to be drawn into other conversations had we stayed with so many other people.

She looked at me and softened a little more, saying, 'We can go anywhere you want.'

My room was not very large and had two single beds with a night table in between. Peter's bed was closer to the window and stood next to the only chair. Not wanting to sit on his bed, I motioned Jane to sit next to me on the edge of mine.

'I know something is up with the Duchess and would really appreciate it if you gave me a hint before the meeting tomorrow.'

'It is something to do with your German charity,' was Jane's reply. 'I think that Her Royal Highness feels that she really does not have enough time to devote to it at this point.'

'But last week when I visited her at Kingsbourne [Sarah's new home] she promised that she would make a commitment to its success.'

'That is really all that I know,' said Jane, and then added, 'I am sorry.'

As she said the last words her voice dropped and got a little husky. She met my eyes, and smiled sadly. We had been sitting inches apart, and as we spoke she had slid closer, so that her right thigh and arm were touching me. I still wonder why I chose that night, after so many opportunities. Perhaps it was the eerie music, which somehow fit the feeling I had that something was dying in my relationship with Sarah. Maybe seeing vestiges of the old Jane reminded me of happier times – or maybe it was the disturbing story of the driver.

I meant to simply kiss her on the cheek, but as I turned, my arms encircled her narrow waist and I found myself kissing her fully on the mouth. There was no resistance. I suppose that she expected it. Her arms wrapped around me and her eyes closed. Jane opened her lips to my kiss and then plunged her tongue roughly into my mouth. Despite the large slit of her skirt Jane's dress was too tight to allow her to straddle her legs around me, and so she leaned her weight against my chest and, guiding me with her arms, pushed me down onto the bed, sliding over me and grinding her hips. Her mouth remained clamped on me and her lips pressed mine harshly.

As I lay on my back Jane continued grinding against me and, freeing one arm from behind me, ran it down the side of my chest towards my thighs. All the while her hips continued their rhythm. Arching her back she raised her torso slightly and snaked her free hand onto my chest, yanking roughly at the tuxedo studs which held the shirt shut. One golden fox-headed stud flew across the room as her hand slipped onto my skin, sliding down until the cummerbund arrested her passionate progress. 'Ugh,' she sighed as she pulled on the band, actually ripping the Velcro that fastened it in place. Jane knew her way around men's clothing, and her well-trained hands quickly unfastened and began to unzip my trousers. That is when the situation became a little comical.

You see, I was wearing a pair of black braces which had tiny loops that fitted very tightly over the waist buttons of my trousers. Even with time and a steady hand it was not easy to unbutton them. In our current state of excitement, it proved impossible for Jane. She pulled, twisted and tore, grunting with growing frustration. Finally losing patience, she slid down to the floor and held the flaps of my trousers open, like a surgeon clamping open an incision. She then pulled the trousers apart as far as the elastic of the braces would allow before burying her head in the opening.

I raised my head to watch the determined look on her face before it vanished between my legs. And God help me if I could not resist saying, 'Jane, you are finally giving me a penguin!' Unperturbed by my levity, she continued with fierce determination and over-abundant (almost painful) enthusiasm. Naturally it was not unpleasant, but I was conscious of a sense of over-compensation – as if she were trying to prove how good she was. Conscious that Peter might return at any moment and concerned that she could not possibly maintain her current tempo indefinitely, I sat upright on the bed and reaching down, pulled Jane upwards and on top of me. I rolled over, freeing my weight, and slid Jane's skirt as high as I could. Then, grabbing at her tights and pants, I pulled them down to her knees. I did this roughly, staring down at her the whole time. Then, pulling her legs apart (as much as the elastic of her pants would allow), I climbed between them.

I know that this should be an erotic memory, but my strongest recollection of that particular moment is one of the absurdities of my position. I had my back to the door, while the strong elastic of the braces held the back of my trousers in their normal place. On top of this, I had not even taken off my dinner jacket. Jane, too, was fully dressed in black. We were a very formal couple. And so it occurred to me at the time that if Peter were to open the door, the sight with which he would be confronted would be that of two penguins having sex.

Jane performed with as much zeal in this position as she had orally. Yet once again I was left with the impression that it was somehow contrived, or exaggerated; there were anatomical signs which signalled to me that her sincerity might be in question. It is possible that she sensed my scepticism, for she increased the intensity of her movements and the pressure of her lips. As Jane sensed impending completion, her teeth clamped onto my lower lip and at the critical moment bit down roughly. She held my lip between her teeth for several seconds, while her fingers dug through my dinner jacket into my back.

I have always been very proud of my tailor, and when I returned to London I told him of the incident, advising him to use it for advertising. 'Malcolm,' I suggested, 'you could create a poster depicting the scene with a caption saying "You can do anything you like in a Savile Row suit – just remember to unzip it before you begin".'

The moment we were finished Jane pushed me off and slid her pants and tights back into place. She sat on the edge of the bed for a few seconds and then stood up, saying, 'I really must be leaving.' There was no attempt at tenderness, or even an acknowledgement of what had transpired. I was still a little dazed, and my lower lip was throbbing and a little swollen. 'Wait a minute,' I said.

'Yes,' said Jane with a funny little smile, as if she meant to add something sarcastic like 'Will there be anything else, sir?'

'Well, Jane . . . we used to be such good friends . . .' I am not sure what I was searching for, or what I was really trying to say, except that I missed Jane Dunn-Butler very much. Earlier that evening I had seen a glimpse of the sweet girl I had described so warmly in my diary of our first meeting, the romantic, innocent girl who had saved her pennies to buy me a copy of *Wuthering Heights*; how could she have come to this, I wondered. I wanted to talk to her, to see if this strange creature even remembered who and what she once was.

Lady Jane interrupted my thoughts, announcing impatiently once more, 'I really must be going.' There was no emotion, not one spark of humanity left in the cold, shark-like eyes which stared blankly back at me. She walked towards the door in some haste, not even stopping in the bathroom to freshen up. It was clear she had another place to go, now that she had concluded this piece of unfinished business.

'Jane!' I almost cried out her name

She paused with her hand on the doorknob, staring at me with a little curiosity.

'What happened?' I asked.

Suddenly her face contorted into a horrible look of warped triumph. With her mouth still twisted in a cruel, bitter grin, she turned her head coyly to one side, and said simply, 'You missed your chance, Allan.' And with that she was gone.

I sat on my bed, dishevelled and depressed, with the taste of my own blood in my mouth. That was the last time I was to see Jane, until we would meet again in the dock of the Old Bailey.

CHAPTER TWELVE

JANE ANDREWS AWAKENS FROM HER ROYAL DREAM

THE NEXT DAY would bring the final step in the ascendancy of Lady Jane. As I have pointed out, the victors in the Court of Fergie were those that survived the longest. Sarah had tried to coax me away from John Bryan and when I refused she simply made other plans, which were announced at the 'breakfast meeting' – plans that I simply would not accept. As I listened to Sarah withdraw from a number of commitments to which she had pledged herself, I decided to end my relationship with the Duchess of York.

Lady Jane was to be the direct beneficiary of the vacuum left in the spheres of influence in my absence. The following two years would be a time of great success and then devastating failure for Lady Jane. Her love life would be a dramatic departure from the unfulfilled longings, then secretive wanderings of bygone days. Her relationship with Sarah would reach new levels of intimacy – but she would suddenly experience the most profound rejection of her professional life.

Soon after the trip to Poland, Jane came out of the closet with her adulterous love life. She made no secret of her relationship with the dashing and socially well-connected Dimitri Horne, and moved into his Kensington flat six months after their dramatic meeting. Christopher Dunn-Butler first separated from Jane, and then filed for divorce citing adultery as the cause. The mismatched marriage, which had lasted seven years, was over. With the loss of Christopher,

Lady Jane effectively severed her last tangible and publicly visible tie with her humble past. Christopher had begun dating her when she was just a timid servant in Buckingham Palace. He had rescued her from her virtual poverty, and had given her an enhanced social legitimacy. But Jane had outgrown Christopher and hungered for much more. He was cast aside and they would maintain an infrequent correspondence until Jane came to need his help once again.

An interesting addendum regarding Jane's early days with Christopher was made public after the trial, and sheds enormous light on Jane's character as well as the couple's interaction. When Christopher first met Jane on a vacation in Tenerife, he was living with a woman named Patricia Muirhead. Christopher was enamoured with Jane and almost immediately ended his relationship with Patricia. He bought Patricia out of the flat they shared, but a dispute began over some jointly owned furniture. Shortly after the incident Pat received a box of chocolates. She recalls: 'The chocolates came in a light-coloured half-pound box with a little note in wobbly handwriting. It said:

> "Dear Pat, you are such a sweet person." After a dinner to celebrate my birthday I handed them out. My daughter and a girlfriend of mine each took one . . . within seconds the girls spat them out, saying they tasted "mouldy". We had a look and saw evil-looking turquoise stuff inside. There were dozens of little pellets and someone said "My God Patricia, that looks like rat poison" . . . They were analysed later and that's exactly what it was.

The blood-thinning agent used in rat poison can produce a fatal brain haemorrhage and massive internal bleeding in humans. Naturally, Patricia turned the evidence over to the police, who then interviewed Jane and Christopher. No charges were brought, but the inspecting officer told Patricia that he suspected Jane knew something about the poison.

After the trial it was also revealed that prior to meeting Jane, Christopher Dunn-Butler was simply known as Chris Butler – it seems part of Jane's early metamorphosis required the 'upgrading' of her married name. Patricia recalled, 'Jane was a terrible snob even though she was an ordinary girl from Grimsby . . . Chris was plain old Chris Butler when I knew him . . . but I don't think Jane thought that was posh enough for Buckingham Palace so they became the Dunn-Butlers. I think Dunn is a family name on Chris's side . . . It was ever so funny because my friends and I couldn't help but call him Chris Dung Beetle from that moment on.'

Clearly being a 'Dung Beetle' held only limited charm for the ambitious Lady Jane, and the securing of Dimitri Horne as an appropriate consort seemed to be of the utmost importance to Jane's plan.

Difficulties soon began in the relationship with Dimitri. He began to complain of the same type of symptoms that had concerned me, and would ultimately destroy her relationship with Cressman. Dimitri recalls that, 'I always felt that she would be following me wherever I went – I was not able to go and visit a friend without her trying to track me down.' Finally, Dimitri could not take her moodiness and obsessive behaviour any more and decided to end the relationship. Ironically, the couple was on holiday when he announced his decision. The similarities to the South of France holiday in which Thomas would come to a similar decision are very great. The only difference is that Dimitri and Jane were in Greece. When he told her that it was over, she attacked him. Dimitri recalls, 'She turned violent, punching and kicking. I was actually afraid, because when she became violent she was totally unpredictable.'

Finally Dimitri was able to move Jane out of his Kensington flat. It seems to have been a traumatic experience, and a costly one. Lady Jane was not willing to lose this new, socially prominent lover, and began to stalk him. Dimitri recalls, 'She was basically stalking me, coming to my house at awkward hours, ringing the doorbell, and calling me at work. One evening I went out with friends to a ball at the Grosvenor House Hotel. She must have been following me, because she left all sorts of messages on my car windscreen . . . they were pleading messages. Pleading with me to come back.'

It is perhaps only a quirk of fate that it was Thomas and not Dimitri who lost his life at the hands of Jane. At one point Dimitri allowed Jane back into his flat and she went berserk: 'I let her in, hoping to maybe just talk to her, and she went crazy, started punching and kicking me. She was throwing things at me.' Dimitri's brother was in the flat and together they were able to calm her down. Dimitri was quite protective and kind toward Jane's reputation at the time, but it is reported that she had actually attacked him with a pair of scissors.

Lady Jane returned one last time to collect her belongings. When Dimitri returned home he thought that he had been burgled. A number of his favourite possessions were missing, including a valuable Bulgari wristwatch and an oil painting. He was even more astonished to learn several days later that £8,000 had been paid from his brother's current account to Jane. Dimitri speculated that Jane 'must have gone into his [brother's] room, found his cheque book and forged his signature'. This is odd behaviour for a woman responsible for the credit cards and current account of a duchess. When Dimitri threatened to complain to Sarah, the money was returned, but Jane kept the watch.

As frenetic and dangerous as her love life had become, Jane had been enjoying ever-greater success in her role with the Duchess. The entire original cast from the transitional days in which Fergie left the royal household had been eliminated. Jane Ambler still maintained a sporadic role, but Lady Jane was the only real survivor from the palace days. Her presence represented a sense of continuity with Sarah's fading royal past. Jane's contacts within the palace still offered the possibility for exchanges of information, and a physical link. In addition, Jane had made the transition from servant to member of staff, mirroring Sarah's own transition from civil list royal to businesswoman. The two ladies had gone through a major change together, and would finally even consummate their divorces at almost the same time.

The tabloids photographed the two ladies together ever more frequently. Their appearances blurred together to the point where they looked more like twins than Sarah and her own sister, Jane Ludecke. At least this part of Jane's life seemed to be going smoothly. Then disaster struck.

Despite her transformation, Lady Jane still maintained her humble duties as dresser. These duties included responsibility for Sarah's wardrobe during trips. On a visit to America in December 1995, a bag carrying the diamond necklace that the Queen had given Sarah disappeared. The necklace was valued at £250,000 and carried enormous sentimental value. It was determined that it had been checked in, unlocked, to the normal baggage compartment of the aircraft. Jane was distraught. The chances seemed small that the necklace would be recovered, but the FBI and the New York police worked around the clock and astonishingly were able to recover the valuable piece, although the diamonds had been separated from the necklace.

Naturally, an incident of this magnitude received daily headline coverage, and Jane was labelled the 'gem of an employee' that lost the Queen's necklace. She was painted as a forgetful and unreliable servant. The Duchess stood by her, and tried to share the blame. But the smirch on Jane's competency would follow her for the rest of her career.

Somehow Lady Jane survived this scandal and remained by Sarah's side for almost two more years. It was Jane's libido and ego, not her lack of attention to detail, that seems to have ultimately cost her the job with which she had defined herself.

It had traditionally been Jane who would reconnoitre and select the homes in the South of France that Sarah rented in the summer. In the late spring of 1997 Sarah selected Jane to visit Tuscany and find her an appropriate summer house.

Jane began her house search that May. While in Italy she met a very dashing count named Gaddo della Gherardesca. He has been described as 'an eccentric Italian aristocrat who lives grandly in Tuscany'. Jane had lunch with Gaddo and the two seemed to experience a spark of interest. At least, Jane believed that an attraction existed, because she told one of her friends later, 'he is interested in me'. She claimed that he even asked her out, 'but I felt it prudent to decline'.

Jane secured an appropriate house and three months later Sarah began her holiday. Soon, she too was lunching with the eccentric Gaddo and quickly, but this time secretly, the Duchess began a relationship with him. It seems that Gaddo still had some interest in Jane − even if it were nothing more than politeness. That autumn, Jane received a postcard from Gaddo, sent to her home. It was a simple and affectionate note, and Jane proudly told one of her colleagues in Sarah's office about it. Two days later she was fired.

Sarah was on a trip to New York at the time, and did not even tell Jane herself. Two other assistants were fired too, and the reason which was given was that it was a cost-saving measure. This simply does not seem possible. When Sarah's overdraft was running wildly out of control, she repeatedly refused to fire Jane. There were times when the Duchess was unable to pay her grocery bills; at one such time I sent her cash in the mail so that she could pay the bill directly. We knew that a cheque would be credited against her Coutts overdraft, and of no immediate use to her. Despite such deprivation, Sarah never considered firing Jane, even hiring Jane's husband. In 1997 Sarah held a press conference in which she announced that she had repaid her overdraft. Is it logical that she would choose her first year free of debt to fire her most trusted employee? It appeared after the dismissal that Jane may have 'fleeced' the Duchess of some money, and taken advantage of her relationship with various clothes designers. But this information was not known in the autumn of 1997; or at least, it was not given as the cause of dismissal. When Sarah returned to England she actually used her connections to find Jane a new job. If she had fired Jane for theft or fraud, she certainly would not have offered her help in placing Jane elsewhere. It is clear from Jane's circle of friends that, at least in her own mind, she clearly believed that the dismissal was a result of the Italian count's interest in her.

Regardless of the events surrounding the dismissal, the loss of her job, her status and her connection with the royal family cannot be overemphasised in importance. Lady Jane lost her title and her identity. The girl from Grimsby had completed her metamorphosis – and had succeeded in modelling herself so successfully after her mistress that she had confused the world, and fooled herself. At one point in Jane's beloved *Wuthering Heights*, Catherine suddenly realises that her identity is so entwined with Heathcliff's that they have become one entity and cries out, 'I am Heathcliff!' Lady Jane had become the Duchess of York. Now the link was suddenly and forever to be severed. Jane was only a reflection, and the mirror was shattered. Without the reflected image of the Duchess there could be no Lady Jane.

Jane Andrews awoke from her dreams of royal life. She was frightened, depressed and alienated from all that she had come to identify as her world. She had come to take the privileges for granted. The gates of Buckingham Palace had been open to her for almost a decade: important people returned her calls, fashion houses welcomed her patronage. In a flash all this was gone.

Jane was devastated. The degree of her loss would even be used during her trial as a mitigating factor in her defence. Suddenly Jane was a nobody once again. Her worst fears had been realised. As a young girl her greatest terror had been the thought that she would end her life working with her schoolmates in one of Grimsby's frozen fish factories. Her former teachers recall how desperately Jane wanted to escape from this humble world. Now her royal dream, and the self-definition it had provided, had ended. Jane Andrews was just a frightened woman with no real credentials, no powerful friends of her own and no clear future. She had turned 30 years old and her life seemed to have ended.

At her trial Jane would speak of this horrible period and her attempts at finding employment. Ultimately, the Duchess used her own connections to secure her a job at Annabel Jones in Beauchamp Place. Sarah had a great deal of clout with the owner.

When that did not work out, Jane was briefly employed at Claridges. Finally she got the job with Theo Fennell. Sarah still maintained a close relationship with Theo — in fact, when he opened a second store in October of 1996 I was asked by Theo to leave the opening reception, for he did not wish to risk upsetting the Duchess. Jane did well with the customers and developed a reputation for hard work. Ironically, after her arrest the police found that she had taken over £12,000 worth of rings and bracelets from her employer. She claimed to have only 'borrowed' the jewellery, but she had never sought permission to do so. This was to be Jane's final position, excluding the jobs she would be given in prison.

Jane's romantic life continued suffering its downturn. Following the end of her relationship with Dimitri, it took Jane almost a full year before she again had a steady boyfriend. She occupied the time with casual relationships, and finally met an insurance broker named Mike Siviter. An insurance broker was a far cry from a Greek tycoon. Still, Jane managed to display her usual obsessive tendencies. Mike followed the pattern that the majority of her lovers would choose — he distanced himself. Jane responded with her pattern, and stalked him in her car.

Next, Jane pursued the friendship she had made during her trip to Kenya with *Daily Mail* journalist Ted Verity. Soon the two were romantically involved and friends reported that Jane was desperate to have Ted's baby. The relationship ended after only four months, when Jane displayed her now-typical pattern of over-obsessive behaviour.

Jane then became involved with an internet executive and this time actually pretended to be pregnant. The stratagem was unsuccessful in clinching a marriage proposal, so Jane was left with the task of disposing of the imaginary foetus. First, she made him aware that she had booked an appointment at an abortion clinic. She then chose a geriatric hospital to simulate the background noise of a hospital, and from there she called her lover to tell him that she had just aborted their foetus. Naturally, she felt that the least he could do was pay for the procedure.

Jane's life seemed to be spiralling downwards. She was in between relationships, unable to hold down a steady job, and behind on her rent, when friends suggested that they introduce her to a handsome and successful young man with his own business in the automotive industry and his own town house in Fulham. Jane met Thomas Cressman in August 1998. A blind dinner date was scheduled at Min's restaurant in Knightsbridge. The attraction seemed to be instant. It is easy to see why; Tommy was dashing, attractive and successful. Not surprisingly, the evening ended in his bed.

Within two weeks Tommy had taken Jane to meet his mother Barbara Cressman at her summer home in the South of France. Within three months the couple had decided to try living together and Jane moved into Tommy's town house. Publicly, it appeared that the relationship was flourishing. Tommy was known for his kindness and generosity. He became aware of Jane's financial distress and helped her renovate her flat so she could let it. He would drive Jane to Theo Fennell's every morning and call her at work during the day. They would leave each other love letters, and Jane would sometimes place a tender note between each of Tommy's shirts as she folded them and placed them in his drawer. She would phone Tommy almost hourly, and if he were not in his office she would quiz his employees on his whereabouts. It reminded me of the Duchess's almost obsessive need for constant telephone contact. Jane seems to have been continuing the eccentric habits she had learned in the Court of Fergie. Tommy tried to help Jane to recover from the loss of her relationship with the Duchess.

Close friends were aware of certain tensions. Tommy's father Harry Cressman was not enamoured with his son's choice, and described Jane as 'not my cup of tea'. She seemed to dwell too much on her glorious past, and would pontificate on the fabulous hotels and places in which she had once stayed. At a dinner party in Harry Cressman's home, Jane was asked, 'Who paid you?' With a pompous sneer she replied, 'The Queen signed my cheque every month.' And so there were signs that Jane might not be the perfect match for the much-loved Cressman. But nobody was prepared for what was about to happen.

CHAPTER THIRTEEN

CASE FOR THE PROSECUTION

He was so good as to take me into the yard and show me where the gallows were kept, and also where the people were publicly whipped, and then he showed me the Debtor's Door out of which culprits came to be hanged.

Great Expectations, 1860

LITTLE HAS CHANGED in the outward appearance of the Old Bailey in the 140 years since Dickens's eccentric lawyer Mr Jagger defended his generation of murderers. But society has changed and Jane was fighting for her freedom, not her life. Nevertheless, the traditions of that revered court have steadfastly defied time and, as my taxi turned into Old Bailey Street, I felt a strange quiver of uneasiness as I gazed upon the famous courthouse.

The main entrance was surrounded by a horde of photographers and television camera crews. They had been cordoned into two opposing regiments, allowing a small path into the building. At last Jane would have her own honour guard; finally Jane would be the centre of the world's attention, all on her own.

On the right-hand side of the building is a tunnel called Warwick Passage. It resembles a Tube tunnel, and cuts through the massive structure to the street behind the courthouse. The tunnel is open to the elements at both ends and its arched interior is tiled in industrial white ceramic. The floor is paved in blocks of grey slate. It is cold, damp and windy in Warwick Passage and today it was crowded, for it houses the entrance to the visitors' galleries. The public is allowed to watch murder trials from a gallery above each courtroom. These small mezzanine rooms only accommodate 30 people, and so it is necessary to queue up for the more notorious trials. After a number of delays, the trial was finally scheduled to begin on Tuesday, 24 April. I was told that it would begin at 2.00 p.m. and by noon the visitors had already begun to arrive.

The crowd expected to be entertained, almost like ancient Romans waiting at the entrance of the Coliseum to see the newest gladiators, and they would not be disappointed. But another drama was about to unfold behind the scenes. As the visitors took their places in the queue, a quiet rumbling began as groups started to speculate over the identity of other groups. An attractive brunette, standing close to a handsome young man bearing a strong resemblance to Thomas, looked in my direction and began to whisper. I could just hear some of their phrases. 'No, I think he is in New York,' said one. 'I heard he is writing a book,' said the other, and both heads shook remorsefully. An attractive elderly couple approached very tentatively. Both were clad in well-worn tan macs. The man looked like the American film star Robert Mitchum, though with greying blond hair. He had Jane's bone structure and her dark-brown eyes. The lady had very blonde hair and deep-blue eyes which seemed glazed with fright. They clung close together, as if they were shielding one another from danger. Both smiled whenever they made eye contact with the crowd. The others looked at them suspiciously and the whispering intensified. I felt a huge pang of pity for Jane's parents. They too were victims, as were the relatives of Thomas – they were the ones left to deal with the consequences of this tragedy.

There were a number of curiosity seekers who came and went, but the nucleus of visitors would remain the same over the course of the trial, and pretty soon they would know the identity of one another. On that first day it was interesting to watch the speculation; I likened it to a wedding, in the sense that one almost expected an usher to ask 'Friend of the bride or the groom?'

As we waited, the wind howled through the passage and we could watch the rain pounding down at both ends of this strange tunnel. It felt as if we were waiting to be admitted to a hospital room, or even to watch a public execution, but it did not feel like the entrance to the halls of justice. All I could see were frightened people.

Frightened of the rules that governed this place, unsure if they would even be allowed in. For all, there was the fear that justice would not prevail; yet there were naturally two opinions of what was just.

In Jane's parents I could see an additional set of fears. They were afraid of how the others looked at them. They somehow seemed to exude a feeling of shared guilt, a sense of apology. Mrs Andrews particularly would jerk her head towards anyone who stared at her and offer a pathetic smile. I felt ashamed of myself for participating and chronicling this human tragedy, and had I not already gone too far I would have walked away right then. It was a feeling that would go away the moment my eyes met those of Jane.

Finally, the light above the entrance door went out and a uniformed guard opened the door. We were herded up a flight of steps, through a metal detector, to another guard who checked to see if we had mobile phones. A thriving business had emerged at the pub across the street where one could leave one's mobile phone for a price. It reminded me of the saloons in Tombstone where cowboys had to leave their six-shooters at the door. After the security search, there were an additional four flights of stairs to climb, and then another wait in a cold stairwell lobby which smelled of strong disinfectant. By now the groups had mingled into a mob. During the period in which we stood single file, the majority of the conversations could not be heard in their entirety. Now there was a continuous babble, and if you concentrated on a particular group, you could overhear some startling things. Many people were not aware of the identity of Jane's parents and I cringed at some of the sentences they must have been overhearing.

They stood on the stairs, two steps below the landing, and simply smiled and clutched one another, exiled in their shame. I wished that someone would tell them that they were not to blame. Who could have known that their daughter would have come to this? They were just ordinary people from Grimsby who had worked hard all their lives and now, at this stage of life, had to be confronted with public humiliation. Jane's father had taken off his mac, and I noticed that he was wearing a blue pinstripe suit. It would be his main garment for the coming three weeks. The suit was old and fitted poorly. His shirt was frayed at the collar and cuffs, and his ancient tie was tied in a large, uncomfortable knot high on his throat. Jane's mother wore a grey suit and brown shoes that somehow did not seem to match. She clutched at her handbag as if it were a lifebelt. Looking at them, I couldn't help but think of Lady Jane's elegant airs and expensive clothes. Had she never given her father a decent necktie? Of all the shirts that she designed and ordered for Fergie's men and her own, could she not have given one to her father? Was her aversion to Grimsby and her roots so strong that she neglected to assist the only people with the courage to stand by her now?

Suddenly the double glass doors were opened and the tall security guard said, 'Court seven'. We hurried through the first oak door on the right and descended into the gallery. Let me describe the scene; the geography is significant. The visitors' gallery has three rows of ten seats. One enters at the top row and can descend along two steps to the middle and lower rows. The bottom row sits against a balustrade which is clad in marble. The entire gallery is bracketed by a massive stone arch cut into the left-hand wall of the courtroom. In a sense, it is exactly like the mezzanine of a theatre, except it is on the left-hand side. The gallery is tucked away about 15 feet above the courtroom, and faces across the three long tables on which the barristers sit, to the right-hand side of the room. This side is divided into two tiered seating areas. Each area is furnished with exactly 12 seats upholstered in green leather. The left end, nearest the judge, is for the jury; whereas the right end is for the world jury – namely, the press. Looking to the far left, from the vantage point of the elevated gallery, one sees the platform upon which the judge is seated. His large green leather chair, below the royal seal, is set at the same height as the top row of the jury box. Along the wall opposite the judge's platform, also elevated to the same level, is a long platform that runs the width of the courtroom. It accommodates eight seats, all in a row. This is the dock where the accused sits.

Much of the interior of the Old Bailey has been renovated. As a result the rooms lack the dramatic old-world charm with which they have been associated in such films as *Witness for the Prosecution*. The old mahogany panelling has been replaced with bleached oak, giving it a contemporary flavour. Nevertheless, the Queen's Counsel still wear their traditional black robes and white wigs. It is a strange throwback to the past, to see such traditional garb in such modern surroundings. It somehow makes one feel that, despite the furnishings, the role of society to police itself has gone on here uninterrupted for 250 years, since the original Bailey was rebuilt after its destruction in the Great Fire of London.

As we entered the gallery, Jane's parents descended to the lower row of seats and walked to the extreme right-hand side of the gallery, so that they would be closest to the dock. I sat behind them in the middle row, and was so intent on finding a place that I did not notice the courtroom was already filled. Only the jury box was vacant.

As I looked down to try to orient myself my eyes wandered to the right, to the dock. As I have pointed out, the dock spans the entire back of the courtroom. Normally, police surround the accused, and often there are a number of accused persons sitting next to one another. But Jane sat all alone in the middle of that empty platform, in the very centre of the dock, thus commanding the entire rear of the courtroom. It appeared as if fate had finally given Lady Jane her own throne – and even a court of her own.

She was dressed entirely in black, like a defrocked nun, or the angel of death. The clothes clung tightly to her slender frame. I suppose that her carefully prepared wardrobe was meant to engender a sense of pity, but to me it simply looked sinister. You might recall that my first impression of Jane's physiognomy was not overly flattering. I had commented on her overly accentuated bone structure. This desperately thin Jane was all bones. Her face was angular and severe, without the softening influence of any make-up. Her hair was stringy and greasy, with patches of thinning hair at the place where she parted it. Her hands were folded in her lap, over the tight black trousers that she would wear each day over tight black boots. She had covered her black turtleneck with a black overcoat. As I looked at her I saw her fidgeting fingers slip into her left pocket and withdraw a crumpled tissue. She drew it to her nose and shook her head downwards, silently blowing into the tissue. All at once, the years apart vanished, for that was one of the few things that was typically and consistently Jane; that strange, soundless, sniffling gesture. I had seen it first on that wonderful day by our *Wuthering Heights* 'Rock' overlooking the Rhine, and a hundred times since. I began to soften; then suddenly Jane looked up. She had meant to smile at her parents and our eyes met. If I could describe that look I wonder how much easier it would be for you to understand her crime. She jerked her head to the right, tightened her features and exuded a sense of loathing, anger, betrayal and contempt so profound and obvious that two journalists immediately noted it.

An aged blonde head, next to Jane's parents, swung around to gaze angrily at me. I had not noticed her before, but she would accompany the Andrews throughout their ordeal. She would wear increasingly outlandish hats, and one began to wonder if she had confused the visitors' gallery at the Old Bailey with the royal enclosure at Ascot.

A security guard remains in each visitors' gallery to ensure that there is no talking and so a hush fell upon us as we prepared ourselves for act one of this tragedy. The first order of business is to select a jury. This is done automatically, and in this case none of the jurors were contested. Oddly, the luck of the draw produced ten female jurors of the 12 selected. There are two divergent opinions about that strange coincidence. Some people believed that women would be more inclined to feel sorry for Jane; while others thought they would be more qualified to see through her wiles.

Each juror must be sworn in, and then the trial commences. Let me give you a brief description of the process. The prosecution is allowed to make their case first. In the opening argument the prosecutor, in this case Mr Bruce Houlder QC, summarises the allegations and even gives a synopsis of the argument for the defence. This allows the jury to view the evidence with both arguments in mind. The prosecutor then builds his case by taking the jury through the chronology of major events in the relationship, and the crime. The crime scene is analysed, with a pathologist's report on the nature of the wounds and a blood-pattern analysis on the clues created by the splatter of blood. The witnesses for the prosecution are then called to give testimony, and the argument for the prosecution takes life. During this process, the defence is allowed to cross-examine these witnesses.

I have offered this detail to create a backdrop for the shocking spectacle that would now unfold. We had come to the Old Bailey to observe the resolution of a capital crime. Instead, we were to see the perpetration of another crime; namely a violent attack upon the reputation of Thomas Cressman. The prosecution would build its case with surprisingly few questions from the defence. Most of the material regarding the chronology of events would remain uncontested. The shocking revelations upon which the defence would build its strange case would come later in the trial.

Bruce Houlder QC began the proceedings by stating the case for the prosecution. He made a long speech in his soothing, slow-paced voice. He categorised Jane as a 'usually friendly and decent person who was so transformed and burnt up inside by her anger that she killed'. I thought the word 'transformed' was well chosen, for it is indeed the premise of this book that Jane had gone through a fatal transformation. Mr Houlder was concentrating on the transformation that occurred during the Cressman relationship, but to understand the complete background of Jane's metamorphosis, one needed to go back considerably further into the past.

The argument of the prosecution went on to describe the killing as 'no sudden crime of passion', but alleged that 'she killed him when she realised their relationship was simply not going to last and her hopes of marrying him evaporated . . . as the heat went out of their relationship, anger and jealousy rose up in her and she took terrible revenge on the man she truly loved'. Then, softening and motioning towards Jane as she sat quietly in the dock, Houlder went on to say, 'Perhaps afterwards she was appalled and quite frightened by the violence she had shown.' The prosecution then outlined the glaring number of lies with which Jane's previous statements had been peppered. He pointed out that she 'first knew nothing about the killing and then acted in self-defence'. After the completion of his statement he began to tell us the strange story of Jane's involvement with Thomas.

The relationship had begun two years earlier, shortly after Jane had lost her job with the Duchess of York. Witnesses were called to recount how devastated Jane was at the loss of her position, as well as her estrangement from the Duchess and the princesses. One of the first witnesses was a man whom Jane had befriended in 1997 while still employed by the Duchess. Gil Hancox described how Jane solicited his friendship over the ensuing months. He categorised Jane's reaction to her dismissal with the following words: 'I think she was devastated at how unexpectedly it happened . . . she became disillusioned about what she possibly could do as a career . . . it had been a very difficult time for Janie . . . her losing the job with the Duchess. I think perhaps she was trying to draw strength from other areas and her relationship was very important to her.'

Gil's assessment of Jane's disillusionment was quite perceptive, considering that he had only had the opportunity of knowing Jane for a small number of months prior to the dismissal. Having observed Jane's metamorphosis, I would have to say that 'devastated' is an understatement.

As friends of both Thomas and Jane were called, a picture began to form of their relationship. It seems that although the couple were seriously involved, Jane was considerably more certain that she wanted a future together than Thomas seemed to be. Thomas's best friend, Richard Gore, described Jane as 'an intense character, intense about getting married and intense about catching Tom'. But he pointed out that Thomas 'was not ready for marriage, not to Jane'.

It appears that serious problems began within the first year of the relationship, when the issue of Jane moving in to Thomas's house was first addressed. Gil Hancox went on to explain, 'They had been arguing about moving in together . . . things between them were breaking down.' The couple seemed to recover from this troubled period and decided to try living together. Jane let her flat in Battersea and moved into Thomas's town house in Maltings Place. For a short period of time the relationship seemed to stabilise, but then there were a series of additional setbacks. At one point Jane moved out of the master bedroom and occupied the guest room one floor above, for a number of weeks. Again the couple reconciled and Jane returned to Thomas's bed.

A major incident took place in May 2000, just four months prior to Thomas's death. His friend John Gore (another close friend, bearing the same family name) had invited Thomas to a stag night in Berlin. Moments after Thomas departed for the trip, Jane turned on his computer and looked through his personal correspondence. It reminded me of the time that Jane had found my diaries of the Victoria trip on Sarah's desk and had read the parts I had written about my feelings for her. This time, however, Jane's curiosity was rewarded with a shock: she discovered a series of e-mails between Thomas and an American woman in Las Vegas named Deborah. E-mail is a strange symptom of the computer age, and offers a snooping person the unprecedented opportunity of viewing both outgoing and incoming messages. As a result, Jane was able not only to learn what Deborah had written to Thomas, but also to view the highly sexual missives Thomas had sent back to her. In addition to the strong sexual content, at one point Tommy described Jane in unflattering terms: 'The girlfriend's getting a little like a pair of old slippers I can't throw away.'

Jane was irate and hurt. She immediately called and left a message on Thomas's mobile phone, as well as the phones of his group of friends. When they landed in Berlin the messages were waiting for them. After the trip Thomas tried to assuage the damage that his letters had caused. The couple reconciled, but the scar of that shock would haunt Jane. Her innate insecurities were awakened and her natural distrust of men was focused relentlessly on Thomas.

One month later, in June, during John Gore's wedding reception, Jane overheard Gore inviting Thomas to spend an evening in Brussels. The two men were planning on producing a film together and needed to visit some associates there. It would have been inconvenient to try to fit the trip into one day and John suggested that they take an afternoon train and spend the night in Brussels. When questioned about Jane's reaction to this conversation, John Gore recalled: 'I made a casual remark about sorting out the trip to Brussels. Jane's face – it's difficult to explain, but she was obviously furious. It was a horrible look, quite frightening.'

I have seen that look on Jane's face and agree that it is very difficult to explain. It is exactly the same way she looked at me on the first day of the trial when she saw me seated behind her parents. She has a way of snapping her head away from you and then slowly looking ahead, as if she does not wish to acknowledge that you exist. All the while a sense of pure suppressed fury seems to exude from her. Thomas respected Jane's wishes and abridged the trip to one day; but the two friends were destined never to produce that film. When Gore was asked why he believed that Cressman had remained with Jane, he responded that Cressman 'inherently did not want to do anything horrible'. This was a very different Thomas Cressman from the one that Jane would soon try to describe.

Apparently Thomas's attempts at placating Jane were successful, for the relationship continued and friends even began to speculate that a wedding announcement might be forthcoming. The couple spent the early part of the summer looking for a weekend home in the Cotswolds. Thomas even insisted on a 'granny annex' so that his mother could spend time with them. It seemed as if the relationship were back on track.

Jane spent a great deal of time preparing for their summer trip to the South of France that September. Her colleagues at work noticed that she seemed tired and strained. Nevertheless, the couple flew to Barbara Cressman's summer home the first week in September.

By all accounts the trip started well. The couple took Thomas's vintage, mahogany Riva speedboat by trailer to Italy, and spent three fun-filled days together. This was apparently the high point of their trip, and indeed they both regarded it as 'the best trip ever'. But things went very wrong upon their return to Barbara's home. On Friday morning, 15 September, the couple woke up in a troubled mood. They spent the early part of the day shopping in St Tropez, where they quarrelled. Barbara Cressman recalls that Jane seemed put out by suggestions that came from Thomas, and kept saying, 'It's always about Tommy . . . everything must be for Tommy.' They spent the later part of the morning shopping alone, and upon their return to the villa the tension between them was very apparent. When asked to describe Jane's demeanour upon her return to the villa, Barbara said 'she appeared like a thundercloud'.

Jane sequestered herself in the guest room and even refused to join the family for lunch. Thomas had lunch with his mother and nephew David, and then spent the afternoon in the guest room with Jane. The couple was scheduled to fly back to London that night, and drove to the airport with Barbara and David. David was booked to depart on a later flight, but needed to change his ticket. According to Barbara Cressman, even the necessity to leave for the airport sooner than planned, in order to reissue the ticket, upset Jane.

In the car the atmosphere was tense. Jane sat next to Tommy, who was driving, and spent the entire time on both of the couple's mobile phones. She called her mother as well as a number of her friends, essentially using the conversations to bait Tommy. Jane expressed her disappointment with her relationship and told her friends that she had wasted two years of her life. We know from Jane's ex-husband Christopher that she called him at this time and 'she said that she'd had a nice holiday but that it had ended up with disappointment from her point of view, as it looked like Tom did not want to marry her . . . she was obviously upset that this was the outcome . . . deeply upset'. Tommy remained quiet throughout the car journey, but his nephew noted that Tommy's face in the rear-view mirror, and noticed it looked strained. Even the choice of a parking spot seemed to anger Jane, who reiterated her theme of the day that 'everything was for Tommy'.

In the airport Jane continued to query Tommy about their relationship and periodically began to cry. At one point, on an escalator, David noted that Tommy finally lost his temper and slightly raised his voice to Jane, asking her to 'stop messing about'. Other than that, he appeared to simply want to distance himself from her and actually boarded the plane alone.

Jane had been occupied with continuing her general distress calls to her network of friends. It was so reminiscent of the way that Sarah handled crises in her personal life that it seemed that Jane still lived partially in her Sarah persona: I mean that the compulsive use of mobile phones to constantly update a network of friends regarding the minute-by-minute fluctuations of deeply personal issues was typical of life within the Court of Fergie.

Finally, Jane seemed to notice Tommy's absence and asked David if he had boarded without her. She seemed very upset by his answer and managed to enter the plane seconds before the door was closed. By all accounts it was a troubled flight. The runway in London had been closed and the trip took considerably longer than planned. We will never really know what was discussed during the journey. Jane claims that Tommy finally agreed that he needed the help of a psychotherapist to help him with his 'black moods' and fear of commitment. Whatever might have been said, the couple returned to Tommy's house in Maltings Place still together, and according to Jane they made love that night. Jane's words imply that the relationship was back on track and that the future was bright and promising.

In the recent Academy Award-winning film *American Beauty*, the protagonist says, 'The only day that is not the first day of the rest of your life is the day that you die.' Saturday, 16 September, would be that day for Tommy Cressman. A great deal of the events of that tragic day have been pieced together as a result of information gathered from the recipients of the many telephone calls that were made. We also have Jane's version. Sadly, we will never know what Tommy might have said to explain the events of the day.

Jane was not feeling well and was scheduled to go to work that day at her employer's jewellery store, Theo Fennell. Tommy called on her account and explained that she had not slept well and was feeling very ill. He then crossed the street and spent a great deal of the morning working in his office. During this time Jane made calls to local psychotherapists and even a hypnotherapist. She explained that they sought couple therapy. After interviewing them over the phone, she actually made an appointment with a therapist located in Islington. When Tommy returned from his office he cancelled the appointment, explaining that Islington was too far away. Jane was apparently very disappointed by Tommy's reaction to her proactive attempt at seeking therapy. Apparently another argument erupted and, according to Jane's account of the day, it turned violent. We can be sure of one thing; it is clear that Tommy felt he needed help, because he called the police. The conversation he had with the emergency services was fortunately recorded and the text was read to us during the trial. It is clear from this call that Tommy was scared someone would get hurt, and that he desperately wanted Jane out of his home immediately. The following is a transcript of the conversation:

> Operator William Pearce answers, and asks if there is a problem.
> *Cressman*: Yeah, I am having a major fight with my other half.
> *Operator*: Anyone injured?
> *Cressman*: Not yet.
> *Operator*: Where is the other half?
> *Cressman*: Staring at me. One second . . . [Female voice in the background shouting. Footsteps heard running to the telephone] . . . we are rowing and someone's gonna get hurt unless . . .
> *Operator*: What do you want the police to do?
> *Cressman*: I would like the police to come and split us up. She's picked up the other line.
> *Operator*: What do you want us to do?
> *Cressman*: I would like someone to stop us hurting each other. If we don't have somebody here soon somebody is . . .
> *Operator*: What's the argument over?
> *Cressman*: Our relationship. I would like to discuss it, calm down. She will not.
> *Operator*: What do you want her to do? Leave?
> *Cressman*: Yes.

Operator: You should arrange suitable accommodation for her
to move into.

Cressman: I would love to do that.

Operator: That's something you will have to discuss calmly.
There's nothing specifically we can do. We are not a
guidance service. We don't have guidance officers. We deal
with crime. You are best to walk away just now and calm
down and be able to discuss it with her.

Cressman: That's what I have been trying to do.

Operator: If you do require the police, do call us back and, in
the meantime, I advise you to discuss the matter calmly.

We know that shortly after this call was made, Tommy again
returned to his office across the street. The activities that transpired
between these two events are absolutely critical in interpreting the
ensuing events of the day. I will save Jane's sensational version for
later on, when she was given the opportunity to tell it.

When Tommy returned home from the office he found Jane faxing
documents to a number in America. It appears that Jane was very
upset and had decided to disseminate copies of Tommy's e-mail
correspondence with Deborah to a number of people. Jane had
enclosed these missives, along with letters that Tommy had
apparently written in answer to various personal ads, in envelopes
and would later mail them individually to Tommy's parents.
Fortunately, Tommy had the foresight to warn his mother. Barbara
recalled Tommy's call, in which he told her that Jane would be
sending her a bundle of filth and she should just bin it.

Ironically, around the time that Jane was composing her poison-
pen missives, Tommy had also written a letter. While inspecting the
crime scene the police found the very moving words which
described Tommy's feelings for the woman who was about to end his
life. It was torn into tiny pieces and placed in a litter bin. The letter
went like this:

Dearest Janie,

I do care about you. Times have been difficult over the last
few years. I do like you and like being with you. However,
over the last few months I have felt that I have been walking

on eggshells all the time. Your mood swings are so hard to predict. I have tried and tried to make you happy. I do things for you but it never seems to be enough. The jealousy has gotten out of hand. [He then shifts to a reference about a harmless drink he had with a female friend.] I wanted to see Isabelle for a drink, I have known her since we were 24. I just felt worried you would always be asking me ten million questions, when all she is is a childhood chum I bump into every few years. You question me every day and will not let me do anything with the boys and without you. This has just gotten too much. It's my fault for not being harder towards you. [He then refers to the trauma she felt as a result of being fired by the Duchess.] I do realise the hard times you have had and wanted to make things better. What I said over the last few days may seem like total rejection. It's not. You have to sort out these problems you have that go back such a long way. Your insecurities and jealousy are not things you can change over time. They take a lot of work. I can only do so much. You are special and you must realise that. You must make yourself better before putting so much faith in someone else. A couple is two halves, not one whole or three-quarters and the other makes up the rest. I do not think I'm all that great. But you have been making me all of your life and it's too much pressure on me. I must be part of your life and not all of it. The same for you. I do hate to see you so upset. Whatever I say is wrong. I do care!
Tommy XXX.

I think that this letter speaks volumes. It comes from a sensitive man who is frustrated yet still caring and appears to have been written in answer to a prior letter or conversation in which Jane accused Tommy of 'not caring', and perhaps of not wanting to be with her. The letter had been written on notepaper with the letterhead of Barbara Cressman's villa in the South of France. We will never know how it found its way into the garbage in tiny pieces; whether that was Jane's response to the words, or perhaps her way of trying to destroy a letter which depicted her lover as a decent, kind and patient man. That would clearly be a description which would be at odds with the Thomas Cressman Jane wished to portray.

As one might suppose, the now escalating argument resumed with Tommy's return from the office and Jane apparently left the house in a suicidal rage. Jane had developed a pattern of suicidal behaviour over the past two years. She was even hospitalised for it at one point. Dr Sam Marks, a noted psychologist, explained Jane's behaviour: 'During a period of extreme emotional crisis in a relationship typified by turbulence, the frustration level can cause an outburst of extreme violence. Whether the violence is directed internally in a suicidal manner or externally is purely situational, and virtually analogous.'

Jane drove off and again utilised her time alone to notify a large number of her acquaintances that she was having a crisis. She made it clear that this time she really believed that Tommy was finished with her and would never marry her. One of the witnesses for the prosecution was Bridget Cave, a friend to both Tommy and Jane. She was one of the people whom Jane called during her afternoon drive. Bridget was not a very talkative witness, and one got the feeling that she was not overly forthcoming with her answers. Nevertheless, she remembered that Jane ' . . . was monosyllabic, numb . . . she said that her relationship with Tommy was finished. I think it was quite obvious from her voice that she felt angry, betrayed. She referred to affairs Tommy had had, she called him a bastard . . . he wasn't going to marry her.'

Jane then called her cousin and former bridesmaid Andrea Cole, and said that they had broken up. It is important to ascertain that Jane really believed that the tempestuous relationship was over – that this time it truly was finished. The prosecution needed to establish that her feeling of loss and rejection provided a strong enough motive for murder. Later Jane would refute that the relationship had ended, and so the conversations she had during this period are very significant.

While she was gone Tommy was able to make his last call to his best friend Richard Gore. Richard recalls that, 'He sounded stressed and hassled and on the day before said Jane had asked where their relationship was going when they arrived back in England. He said something to the effect that he didn't want to get married and was having second thoughts and as a result of that she had left in her car that morning. I asked if she had packed her bags. He said no, she had just driven off and was going to kill herself. There had been several conversations on her mobile and he was confident she hadn't killed herself . . . I said that she was too excitable and if they got married it was the sort of situation that was going to occur every time they had a disagreement.' Tommy then told Richard that he had even called the police for help. When Richard inquired as to the outcome, Tommy responded with a horribly prophetic phrase: 'They are only interested if there is a body bag.' In a short period of time Tommy's butchered corpse would be removed in exactly that manner.

After refuelling her car at a service station, Jane again returned to Maltings Place, where Tommy was awaiting her. She would later recall that Tommy was very kind at first, and then apparently flew into a rage when she broke a drinking glass. During the ensuing hours Jane would periodically call her ex-husband Christopher. This was odd, since she had contacted him only sporadically since their divorce five years earlier. At one point she called to say that Tommy had attacked her, then later left a voice mail with the reassuring words, 'Don't worry, everything is okay.' Later that Saturday he received a text message which read, 'Hi. It's Jane. I'm really sorry you have been party to everything. It's not fair. It seems to be the story of my life drawing other people into things.' She continued to call him throughout the night, becoming 'more and more upset as the calls went on', but Christopher pointed out that 'having known Jane a number of years she could get upset about things'. He categorised her as 'overdramatic, melodramatic'.

Whatever might have then transpired, one thing is very clear: the two remained together for the rest of Tommy's life. He apparently lay in bed and watched television from about 10.00 p.m. onwards. It was, after all, the summer Olympics. Some time late in the night Tommy was murdered.

The prosecution's claim was that Jane was a woman who, scorned and desirous of revenge, planned and executed a classic murder. Tommy's sight was so poor that one of his friends pointed out 'he could not even brush his teeth without his lenses'. Jane lay next to him, waiting until Tommy had taken out his lenses. He would not have been able to watch television without either spectacles or contact lenses, so it is pretty clear that she waited for him to finish watching the Olympics and prepare for sleep.

Perhaps he was asleep or dozing when she attacked. The blow to his head with the cricket bat was severe enough to expose the bone, and certainly would have stunned him. He even suffered a hairline fracture to the skull. The prosecution alleged that she then plunged the razor-sharp blade of the kitchen knife into his chest. She then left him to bleed to death in the darkened room and after placing two pillows over his head tied the bedroom door shut with the cord of her bathrobe. The knot on the banister was very loose and would have been no obstacle to Tommy, had he really been able to escape his death chamber. The prosecution believes that this was an attempt to create the illusion that she was frightened. Mr Houlder asked the jury: 'Has there not been a measure of rigging of the crime scene? She must have been confused and depressed and in quite a state, and it was a half-hearted attempt to make it appear at least that she was frightened of the man . . . she claimed that she didn't think he was hurt. If that were so, one wonders why she tied the knot so inadequately, because it would not have prevented him from coming out, and why she stayed in the house for a long while afterwards . . . this is highly relevant, when you come to consider whether she is telling the truth. She is saying she didn't realise Mr Cressman was seriously hurt: so what did she think the blood was all about?'

At this point Mr Houlder brought out the bloodstained cricket bat and the knife. They were both exhibited in cardboard boxes with a plastic display window, but even within such innocuous containers they looked evil. The handle of the knife was black, and its long blade was sharp at the edges and the tip. The bat was darkened and its blade was smeared in blood. The jury stared pensively at these weapons of destruction.

The prosecution then took the jury through the series of communications that Jane had initiated during the three-day period when she was on the run. It began with two nebulously worded letters to her parents, which were found at the scene of the crime:

> My dearest parents, I am so sorry. No more hurt inside me any more. Jane X

> Tommy hurt me too much. He was so cruel.

What do these notes mean? Jane explained that she had written them on Saturday afternoon and left them out to scare Tommy. Is that the truth, or were they written after the murder, when Jane was rigging the crime scene to create the image that Tommy was a threat to her?

She then sent an amazing number of text messages to a variety of people, sometimes actually calling them as well. The list included the Duchess of York, Christopher Dunn-Butler and Lucinda Sharp, to whom a large number of messages were sent. The messages tell a strange story. Jane simply pretended that she knew nothing of the crime. She tried hard to create the impression that she had not seen Tommy since Saturday afternoon: she expressed concern and surprise that the press was looking for her, and then feigned shock and horror upon hearing of Tommy's death. Her next step was to create a false trail. She created the story that Tommy had been blackmailed and told her friend Lucinda to tell this story to the police. I will include the text of a number of these messages to give a sense of the level of Jane's deceit; or as Mr Houlder put it, 'an indication of her capacity to lie'.

Tuesday, 19 September 2000

After stopping in Penzance to buy a thong and bra, she sent Christopher Dunn-Butler a message saying:

> Four days now and Tommy hasn't called me. Why?

Then another message to Christopher, at 5 p.m.:

> What's wrong? All the press want me.

7.15 p.m. to Lucinda Sharp:

> Please look after Mum and Dad for me. I am innocent.

8.00 p.m. to Lucinda Sharp:

> All the newspapers have left messages. Please tell them I haven't done anything. I left him on Saturday afternoon. He was okay when I left. I am upset. I can't come back, no one will believe me. I will not be locked up. I must die and be at peace. I love Tommy. I would not harm him, ever.

At 10.07 p.m. Jane sent a text message to Lucinda which the prosecution categorises as a 'complete lie'. The message claims that Tommy was being blackmailed and that Lucinda must tell the police about it.

10.15 p.m. to Lucinda Sharp:

> I am very cold and hungry. I have been trying to talk to my boy since Sunday. What's happened?

11.25 p.m. to Lucinda Sharp:

> I feel cold and sick. Why is someone trying to blame me?

Wednesday, 20 September 2000

12.36 a.m. to Lucinda Sharp:

> I have just heard on the radio that Tommy has been murdered. I can't believe it. I am dying inside.

What was not made public during the trial was that Jane had also tried to convince the Duchess that she was innocent. As the police continued monitoring Jane's mobile, they recognised the number of the Duchess of York. Sarah began the series of text messages by pleading with her former dresser and friend:

> Jane, you must come forward and give yourself up and help the police.

Jane responded with feigned concern over the fate of a mother she had rarely visited during her royal years:

> I'm fine. Look after my mother.

Perhaps trying to keep the lines of communication open, Sarah responded with:

> Give me your mother's number.

At this point, Jane sent Sarah a very similar message to the one she had sent to Lucinda Sharp, pretending to have just learned of Thomas's death:

> I've just heard my boy's been murdered. Can't believe it. All
> fine when I left. Wot's going on?

It appears that Jane lacked the spark of creative genius she had used in her messages to Lucinda, for these attempts at trying to trick Sarah seem to lack a real commitment to her craft. Perhaps Jane felt that the Duchess knew her too well.

At 6.30 that Wednesday morning Jane was found. Lucinda had managed to coax enough information from her for the police to find her asleep in her car at a lay-by in Cornwall. When it was determined she had taken as many as 60 Nurofen tablets, she was transported to hospital. There she was examined and it was determined that her life was not in danger. During the examination no marks were found on her body, and she made no claim that she had been abused, either physically or sexually. After she had fully recovered Jane was moved to London, where she was charged with murder and remanded to Holloway prison.

These events form the skeleton of the chronology of those tragic days. Next, the prosecution provided information about the crime itself, and the scene of the crime.

The jury was given photos of the gruesome crime scene and of Thomas's ravaged body. These gruesome mementos were enclosed in very businesslike black binders. As the prosecution guided the jury through the information, they were asked to look at a particularly horrible photo of Tommy's face. It was meant to illustrate the deep wound inflicted by the cricket bat. Mr Houlder warned the courtroom that people's faces are often not recognisable after death, and said that this was a particular shame as the photo really bore little resemblance to Tommy. There was a hush in the room as the binders were slowly opened to the respective tab. Just as the jury cast their eyes upon Tommy's swollen, battered head, a legal assistant knocked over a large pitcher of water and the liquid seemed to cascade across the room in slow motion. It was a macabre moment, and put everyone on edge.

We are so inundated with books and films about crime that one grows accustomed to discussing violence with some degree of detachment. But now we were confronted with the reality of the human carnage that had been inflicted on a vibrant and happy young man. I looked over at Jane in the dock. She was leaning forward clutching a pen in her right hand. I noticed that she was biting her lower lip. Several journalists were also staring at her – but not one member of the jury would look in her direction.

Mr Houlder began inventorying the long list of wounds which were identified in the post mortem. These injuries included grip marks to the arms that must have preceded the killing by several hours, and indicated a prior struggle. Next, he described the serious injury to his forehead, which had actually exposed the skull. There is a strong possibility that the fracture to the skull was not caused directly by the bat, but by the force of Tommy's brain crashing against his skull. Then there was the gaping hole of about four inches long, along his chest. The blade had actually pierced his right nipple before travelling into his pulmonary sac, skewering his right lung in the process.

Next Dr Nathaniel Carey, the forensic pathologist, gave his findings. The wounds told their own poignant story. Although Thomas's chest contained only one entry wound, in actuality he had been stabbed twice. The blade had entered through the right lung and severed the major arteries and veins supplying the heart. It was then partially withdrawn and reinserted with a downward cutting and slashing motion into the right pectoral muscle. Using a large screwdriver to demonstrate, Dr Carey showed the courtroom the complex set of motions that would have been required to create the internal wounds. When asked if this could have been the result of Thomas falling upon the blade, the pathologist responded firmly: 'The key aspect is that there has been a complex external wound and a complex internal wound, and during the course of that the handle of the knife must have been held quite solidly.' It appears that Thomas's mutilated body served as a silent witness to the truth.

We were then offered testimony from a very specialised branch of forensic science. Apparently the patterns of the splattering of blood also paint a picture of the crime. Dr Kamela de Souza is a specialist in this field and offered us some very startling information. One of her most revealing observations was the fact that blood was found splattered over six feet above the bed. This would indicate that Thomas was kneeling on the mattress when he was stabbed. This would be a very important point when we were allowed later to hear Jane's story.

It had been generally assumed that during the murder Jane was clad in the bloodstained towelling robe found in the bathroom one floor above. Yet, expert analysis of the robe indicated that the bloodstains had originated from the *inside* of the garment! Jane had put on the robe *after* Tommy was stabbed. She had been completely naked as she lay next to him, and naked as she attacked and killed him. His blood had spurted onto her exposed left breast and would later soak through the cloth of the sole garment she would wear – *after* she had completed her evil task. One could almost hear the collective gasp as we imagined the scene.

Even without the benefit of a living witness, the words of the prosecution, supported by the forensic evidence, painted a vivid and eerie picture of a calculated, predatory, almost vampiric slaying. Perhaps the old Jane Dunn-Butler had been influenced by the passions of the Victorian era, but the crime she committed was pure Gothic. One can picture Jane lying in bed next to her relaxed lover. She must have waited patiently for him to finish watching television and remove his contact lenses. Safe and secure in his own bed, next to his lover, Thomas must have dozed off into sleep. Imagine her creeping up to him as he lay propped up on his pillow. She would have been naked, with the heavy, well-used bat held firmly in her right hand. What thoughts were running through her head as she pulled back her hand to brutally strike the skull of her lover? What did she later feel as the blade sank into his chest?

After the murder, Jane was calm enough to clothe herself in a robe, walk out of the room and then pause to tie the door closed. Although she initially claimed that she had run straight out of the house, in actuality she had had the presence of mind to go upstairs and wash, and even to rinse a bloodstained towel. Is this the behaviour of a woman so frightened of her lover that she feels obliged to tie the door shut?

The rules that govern witnesses at the Old Bailey prohibit anyone about to give evidence from sitting in the visitors' gallery until they have spoken. As a result, each major witness would appear among our ranks in the gallery after completing their testimony. It was an odd way to get to know someone, after already seeing them exposed and under oath. By the first Friday of the trial Barbara Cressman had completed giving her evidence and joined us in the gallery. I considered her to be a forthright, elegant and very brave witness, and even before getting to know her held her in great admiration. It must have been agony to listen to such gory details regarding the death of a son who by all accounts was very close to his mother. When I entered the gallery that morning Barbara was already seated in the first row. Exactly six seats to her right sat Jane's mother. I felt a huge pang of sadness for the two ladies. Had circumstances been slightly different, they would have been related; instead, they were joined for life by this link of death. As it turned out one of the jurors had become ill and the trial was postponed until the following Monday. Jane could go back to Grimsby for another weekend.

When we returned, the prosecution was close to concluding its case. The courtroom was shown Jane's first recorded interview, taped on 26 September. By that time, Jane had already altered her original story of not having seen Tommy since Saturday afternoon. She also seemed to have abandoned her earlier diversion of suggesting the possibility that blackmailers had killed him. Now Jane spoke of self-defence. In a small voice, filled with emotion and tearful pauses, Jane played her most convincing role ever – that of Jane the martyr.

She began her soliloquy with the last day of their vacation to the South of France. She recalled that the 'dream' vacation ended with Thomas waking up on Friday morning, the last day of the trip, 'in a really bad mood'.

'We got up really early. I tried to talk to him but he shouted at me. He told me that he never liked to talk before 10 a.m.,' she said.

Apparently Thomas wanted to go to St Tropez, but Jane did not. He appeared 'very stressed and tired' and, as they got ready to go, Thomas accidentally elbowed her in the ribs as they entered the car: 'It really hurt. I said "ouch". He shouted at me and said, "For God's sake, don't be so stupid." I told him that anyone else would have leant over and given me a kiss. I wanted to talk, to find out what we were going to do back in London. Before the holiday we had been to the Cotswolds looking at houses. I was pressing him for an answer . . . he snapped: "I don't know. I need my own space." I replied, "Every time we come to France to spend time with your mother you seem to want your own space." He had gone cold towards me. I began to cry.'

Jane went on to describe the atmosphere back in the villa after they returned from their shopping trip. Thomas went to sit on the terrace and Jane went upstairs to her room to pack her bags. She had decided to confront him again about his lack of commitment. One wonders why Jane was so adamant about resolving their relationship on a day when she clearly felt that he was in a bad mood. '"I understand. You change your mind every five minutes . . ." I said. We argued, but not badly. He went upstairs and came down again in a furious mood. He started calling me names, shouting at me. I tried to ignore him.'

She then describes the scene in the car on the way to the airport, in which she taunted Tommy by criticising him during various telephone conversations to her friends. One wonders if Jane really believed that she could embarrass her lover into being more optimistic about a future together. 'As we drove nobody said anything to me. I asked him what was going on. I picked up the phone to telephone my mum. I wanted to embarrass him and I told my mum that he was up to his old tricks, changing his mind every day. He got more and more angry. His nephew and mother were ignoring it, talking amongst themselves.'

She then was questioned about what transpired at the airport: 'He told me "don't be so stupid, and for God's sake don't cry". I had tears rolling down my face but I was not howling or anything. Then he swung round and hit me. I was embarrassed because it was in front of his nephew and everybody. We went our separate ways.'

Keep in mind that nephew David Cressman was asked specifically, while under oath, if he had seen Tommy hit Jane. He clearly said that he had not seen any violence. In any case, the couple met again inside the aircraft after Jane finally boarded. 'He did not seem to want to talk, but he did in the end. He admitted that he had problems and that we should go and see a counsellor. It was the first time he had ever said he had problems. I said, "Does that mean our relationship has still got a future?" He said, "Yes, but we have got to see a counsellor." I knew he had problems with his parents' divorce, sharing things with anybody and he was very possessive and jealous. I thought it was a breakthrough because it was the first time he admitted he had got problems. We talked. I was still very upset. I did not want to eat anything.'

Jane then described the scene upon their return to Maltings Place late Friday night. 'Things at the house seemed fine. I asked him where he would like me to sleep. He said, "With me, of course." He said he was too tired to talk. We went to bed and cuddled up. We made love.'

The next morning Thomas went to the office and Jane took the day off because she was tired. Jane claims that while Tommy was in the office she leafed through the telephone book and began calling counsellors. The telephone records and even the appointment books of two counsellors confirm this part, at least. Jane appears to have called Tommy's office to tell him she had located a counsellor, and recalls: 'He went into a furious mood when I told him about the appointment. He eventually came back to the house and seemed to have quieted down. He kissed me on the forehead.'

Jane continued her story with her claim that Tommy again lost his temper when he was told that the therapist was located in Islington. It is clear from the therapist's records that a man cancelled the appointment; we can never be sure why. Jane has implied that the therapy was needed primarily for Tommy. She claims that he wanted help with his 'black moods', dealing with his parents' divorce and his sexual problems, but it is odd that Jane would have called therapists and made appointments for the two of them together if the therapy were only needed for Tommy. It is far more likely that they were seeking a mediator for their trouble as a couple. It is also possible that Tommy was ambivalent about this help, if he had already decided against maintaining the relationship. At any rate, Jane recalled that Tommy reacted quite violently. 'He told me that he was not going all the way there. He had suddenly changed his mind again. We started to argue. I said that if he did not want me, I might as well not be here. He said, "Fine, when are you going to kill yourself?" He went into the study and came back with two Stanley knives and a paperweight with a coin on it. He said, "Let's flick the coin and whoever loses kills themselves." I started shouting at him, I said, "Why change your mind again?" and asked if he had been on the internet to the woman in America again . . . he snapped and hit me. I slapped him across the face. He grabbed me by the neck and really squeezed. I pushed him away. I think he realised what he was doing and stopped. He then just ran into the other room and dialled the police.

Apparently Jane ripped out an extension phone from the wall at that moment, then ran downstairs to pick up another extension. If you look back to the transcript of the call, you can see the exact moment that Tommy realised she was on the other line. 'I heard him say "I want her to leave". The man on the other end said that he would have to find me somewhere to live. I put the phone down and he came into the bedroom. I had picked up my mobile. I thought he was going to hurt me. I ran upstairs. I tried to dial a number on my mobile. He hit me again. He said I was not going anywhere. I told him I just wanted to leave and he should let me go. He began trying to throw my bags out of the window. I was telling him that all the neighbours would see. He then just stood at the window. He kept banging his head against it.'

With that, the first tape of Jane's recorded statement ended. There was a hush in the courtroom and it was apparent that the jury was exhausted. The court was adjourned until the next day: the sixth day of this emotional trial had ended. The accusations against the deceased had begun, and they would certainly intensify the very next day.

On the seventh day, Jane created rape.

The moment had finally come for Jane to take the stand. I assume there may have been some debate about the likelihood that her barrister would advise it, but there was never any doubt in my mind. If this entire book should prove one thing, it ought to be that Jane was the consummate actress – of course she would not be denied her most memorable role.

Jane began her performance by creating a general smirch on the character of her deceased lover. She chose to go from the general to the specific, the deductive approach, and most effective. She told of how Tommy had become obsessed with sex in the final months of their relationship. She spoke of his practice of contacting prostitutes during breaks from work, masturbating as he spoke to them on the telephone. She spoke of his demands for kinky sex and clothes, describing how he loved to strap her down on the bed with his ties. Then, after alluding to a fairly undefined history of sexual abuse as a child, Jane delivered the *coup de grâce*. Apparently, after Thomas called the police and practically begged them to get rid of Jane, he forcefully perpetrated an unnatural act upon her. We were asked to believe that as Jane sat on their bed crying, Thomas crawled up and grabbed her legs: 'He started grabbing at me and I was crawling up to the top of the bed. He grabbed hold of my legs. I was hanging onto the brass headboard. I was on my front. He jumped on the bed. He was on top of me, I couldn't move. He grabbed one of the pillows and put it over my head to shut me up . . . he grabbed the cord from the dressing gown I was wearing and grabbed hold of my right wrist. He was so heavy and I was trying to stop him . . . he tied my left wrist to the bed and I was trying to grab hold of him and turning around and spitting at him. I couldn't move. He pulled my dressing gown up and undid his trousers and I just knew what he was going to do, and I couldn't stop him. He pushed himself into me. It hurt so much . . . he just kept laughing at me, saying that he would do something I would really remember.'

Apparently, after completing this alleged anal rape, Thomas simply left the room as she sat sobbing and 'struggled to untie herself'. It seems a rather exaggerated struggle since only her left wrist was supposed to have been tied. Nevertheless, she claims to have 'rushed to the bathroom'. 'I thought I was going to be sick. I just kept pouring water over me,' she continued. Shortly after this Tommy allegedly trapped her in her dressing-room, refusing to let her leave. 'I was screaming at him that I was going to tell everybody, I was going to ruin him . . . I said, "Why did you do that, why?" I said, "If you were the last man on earth I would never marry you now."'

It was at this point that Tommy apparently came into the room with the two Stanley knives and the coin, offering to flip to see who would commit suicide.

Anticipating the obvious question, defence counsellor Kelsey-Fry asked, 'If that is right, why did you not tell the police?'

'Because I was so ashamed, so embarrassed. I just didn't want to talk about it,' was her masterful reply.

Jane continued these revelations, filling in new episodes and conversations to augment the various testimonies she had already provided. She claims that after she 'started screaming', saying she would tell everyone about his 'dirty little habits', she begged him to allow her to leave the house. Although ostensibly burdened with a prisoner in his home, Thomas decided to pop over to the office to do a little more work, leaving his sex slave at liberty to leave. Unperturbed by the incongruity of this situation, Jane proceeded to tell us that she used the time (instead of escaping from her rapist captor) to download sexually explicit emails from his computer. She was apparently caught in the act of her high-tech espionage when Thomas returned from the office and 'started lashing out at me and pushed me into the dressing-room. I was terrified not knowing what he was going to do.' But he left the house again, returning to his office – a rather bizarre pathology for the actions of a vicious jailor and rapist.

Jane justifies her strange reaction by explaining that 'I loved him very much and he had never, never been as violent as he was that morning. Things always used to quieten down after a few days.'

It was at this point that Jane left for her drive of two hours in which she had ample time to call a host of friends. As you will recall from the testimony of those friends, she was monosyllabic and saddened by her belief that Thomas did not want to marry her, and that he really meant it this time. A strange regret to have about one's rapist and, stranger still, she never mentioned either violence or rape during the numerous conversations she had with her friends. On the contrary, she spoke of her conviction that Tommy really would never marry her, that this time it was final.

But returning to Jane's reality: the recently raped Jane conceded to return to Thomas after he begged her to 'come back home . . . he promised that nothing would happen again. I kept asking and asking him, and he promised that he would never do it and that he would get some help. Eventually I decided to go back.'

Prompted by her barrister to ruminate about the wisdom of her decision to return, Jane admitted that 'it was a very stupid thing for me to do and he promised he wouldn't do it again. He reassured me he was going to get help and I wanted to stand by him. I knew from the past that things would blow over.' Yet the noble Jane, now willing to selflessly stand by her man, stood outside the home (in which she had been imprisoned two hours earlier) for about ten minutes, watching Cressman through the window. 'Half of me wanted to go in, the other half didn't. I was frightened about what might happen.'

Tommy greeted her affectionately but soon flew into a rage, as we learned later, when she broke a glass. Somehow he seemed to forgive her even for this, and settled down to watch television in bed. Jane now admitted that she stripped off her robe and lay next to him completely naked. Can anyone regard this as the behaviour of a woman who had been anally raped that very morning – by that very man? Fearing that Thomas might revert back to his perverted ways, Jane made two trips to suitably arm herself for the evening.

The first trip was the result of Jane's assertion that Tommy again tried to have anal sex with her. 'I thought he was just going to cuddle up to me, as he did so many times,' she said, then claimed that instead he tried to initiate anal intercourse. Jane stated that, 'I was pushing him away, saying "don't be so terrible, you said you wouldn't, you promised." He said, "Come on, Janie, you know you like it." I said, "You know I don't." I got out of bed and ran downstairs.'

She returned with a Harvey Nichols cricket bat, placing it on the floor near her side of the bed, and waited for Tommy to sleep. Apparently he awoke and began to argue about a favourite poster that Jane had torn during one of their recent rows. 'He went on about the poster and how horrible I was and he kicked me in the back with his knee,' recalls the woman whose post-arrest physical examination showed no bruises anywhere on her body. 'I got up and went back downstairs. I went to the kitchen and picked up one of the knives. I got back into bed and laid it by the bed . . . eventually I got back to sleep. I woke up and he was hitting me.'

There is clearly some significance in her choice of weapons. To better understand the dynamics of this behaviour, I interviewed Dr Choninsky, a noted psychiatrist specialising in depressive illness. He feels that: 'Miss Andrews' choice of murder weapon was symbolic. Mr Cressman had rejected her as his future wife. Her choice of a domestic instrument . . . from the kitchen from which she would soon be banished should be regarded as symptomatic of her sense of rejection.'

Jane then told the court, 'Eventually I got back to sleep and I woke up and he was hitting me. I got out of bed and picked up the bat and I just hit him . . . he was lashing out at me.' The cause this time was supposedly Tommy's anger that Jane had threatened to expose his perversions and ruin him. Jane recalls that Tommy was kneeling in the centre of the bed, while she was standing naked alongside it as she swung the bat. Apparently the cracking strike of the hard wood only further infuriated him, for Jane went on to say: 'He was pulling my hair out and he was trying to kick me . . . I just grabbed the knife and he came at me. I didn't do anything. He just came at me. He punched me on the back of the head . . . it was dark and I just remember him falling down. I was scared . . . eventually I saw I had blood on me. I was so cold.'

In another interview she provided slightly more information about this battle in the darkened bedroom: 'He was kneeling there grabbing my hair and he started to hammer me. I said, "Don't hurt me." I just stood there because I was so frightened. We struggled. It was so dark . . . he came at me. I had the knife in my hand and that was it. It must have just gone into him . . . I didn't deliberately put it into him . . . he must have just fell [sic] against me.'

Yet while being questioned by Mr Kelsey-Fry, Jane recalled a slightly different version. Although Jane had previously claimed that she asked him not to hurt her during what appears to be a protracted struggle, now she recalled that she did not have the chance to say a word. In her newest version, the stabbing happened too quickly for a word of warning: 'I picked up the knife in my right hand. Tom had hold of my hair. I was trying to hit him with my other hand. I just picked it up because I didn't want him coming near me . . . I didn't have a chance to say anything, he just . . . he was on top of me.'

On perfect cue, defence counsel Kelsey-Fry asked, 'Did you intend that the knife go into Tom?'

'No,' whispered our tortured heroine.

To recapitulate the events according to Jane, Tommy remembered her threats of ruin some time in the middle of the night. Perhaps he had a nightmare about them. He then attacked her without the need for further provocation, and in that darkened room Jane had the time, the cool-headedness and the excellent aim to plant that blow upon his head. Instead of being stunned by the blow, it further incited his anger and he grabbed at her hair and struck her. Now Jane seems to have had time to pick up the knife, but not time enough to warn him that she held it. And in his blind rage he was clumsy enough to fall upon the blade. One wonders how he partially extracted and reinserted it – doubtlessly it was a further act of clumsiness.

Prosecuting counsel Houlder had some questions for Jane during his fairly short cross-examination. When asked why she had not called 999, she answered, 'I was in such a state.'

Houlder cleverly pointed out, 'What about him?', for there was still a chance that Tommy's life might have been saved with immediate aid.

Jane responded that 'he was seriously injured', although she had earlier maintained that she did not know he was badly hurt.

'What did you do – leave him to die?' asked the prosecution.

'No, not at all,' replied Jane. Her explanation was that she panicked and did not think anyone would believe her side of the story. She fled the room and tied the cord of her robe to the door to stop Tommy from coming after her. She did not realise she was covered in blood until she reached the bathroom. She then washed away the blood, dressed and fled towards the West Country.

Finally she agreed that she must have known he was almost certainly dead when she left the house, but she simply could not explain why she did not call for help, why she disappeared for three days, and why she pretended not to know what had happened to him. 'It doesn't make any sense. It's absurd, I know,' the tearful defendant agreed, then went on to explain that, 'I didn't want anyone thinking I had fled the scene and left Tommy to die in that room.'

As the cross-examination continued, Mr Houlder asked Jane some leading questions, including: 'I am accusing you of deliberately killing Tommy Cressman. Did you come with that bat and that knife and strike his sleeping body first with the bat?' I thought that this was an excellent question. You see, there was a very important point in the report of the blood analysis that nobody seemed to notice. The cricket bat was splattered with blood, but the pathologist was certain that it could not have come from the head wound, as it would have taken several minutes for the wound to bleed. In addition, the blood on the bat was splattered while the bat was in motion. The bat was found on the floor by the foot of the bed. None of Tommy's blood had come anywhere near that part of the room. Even Scotland

Yard had to admit that I had a good point when I remarked on this. It means that there is a strong possibility that Jane first stabbed Tommy and then struck him with the bat for another reason, perhaps to create the impression that there was an increase in hostilities, perhaps because stabbing a sleeping person is too macabre. Or maybe Jane attacked him with both weapons in her hands, and was still holding the bat when she stabbed him.. At any rate, I thought that Mr Houlder's question was a good one.

Jane's answer shed no light on my theories, for all she said was 'No.'

Mr Houlder went on to accuse her. 'Then, as he struggled to consciousness you plunged that knife into his chest, striking as accurately with the knife as you did with the bat because he had wounded you by going cool on the relationship,'

'No,' whispered Jane, once again offering no further information.

The prosecution then asked the burning question of why a woman would enter the bed of a man who had just anally raped her hours earlier. Was it 'an act of defiance,' he asked?

'No,' responded Jane.

'Why did you take off your clothes and get into bed with him?' asked the stupefied counsel. 'You were in fear of your life because of what he had done to you that morning, yet you went back to that very place. Why?'

'Because he asked me to,' was Jane's reply.

When asked about the pillows which had been placed over Thomas's head, the prosecution suggested, 'Did you put them there so that you could not see the work you had done?'

'No, not at all,' was Jane's now standard answer.

Jane did later admit under cross-examination that she had told lies to the police about the circumstances of Tommy's death. But she justified these lies by explaining that she was 'frightened' and 'in a state'. She even admitted that the calls and text messages to her friends in which she claimed ignorance of Tommy's fate were 'misleading' and categorised them as a 'smoke screen'.

When again questioned about the alleged rape, Jane reinforced her sentiments of embarrassment and shame. She did add that although Tommy and she had had anal sex together regularly, this was the first time he had forced it on her. I thought that was quite a revelation. Jane had spoken in some detail about the enormous pain the act had caused; yet as it turned out, she was certainly no novice at it.

It became apparent that Mr Houlder was growing frustrated, for he finally exclaimed, 'Things were getting very unpleasant between you, but you have spun it round and suggested the aggression was coming from him when you were the violent one.'

'No,' snapped the monosyllabic Jane.

Jane then appealed to whatever sympathy might be available from the jury box. Speaking of the loss of her job with the Duchess, she said, 'I missed my job. I would say it was a big part of my life . . . it is difficult to explain, to put into words . . . the job lasted for nine and a half years. It was very intense, 24 hours a day, seven days a week. When I lost my job it was a great shock.' She explained that part of the despair that she suffered was the loss of contact with Princesses Beatrice and Eugenie.

She was next asked to describe the sexual abuse that she claimed to have suffered as an eight-year-old child. She had already indicated that it was non-parental, but more information was needed to ascertain what relevance it might have to the case. Jane burst into tears and the judge was forced to adjourn for ten minutes to allow her to compose herself. When she was again asked for specifics, she virtually collapsed and was taken by friends to a waiting ambulance.

After the dramatic end to the cross-examination, the jury was forced to suffer the testimony of the duelling doctors. It seems that in every murder trial, it is obligatory that the prosecution and the defence find respective psychologists to support their case. This would be no exception.

Dr Trevor Turner, consulting psychiatrist for the defence, claimed that Jane's polycystic ovarian syndrome combined with depressive illness would have had a great effect on her moods. 'There would have been swings of mood, a lack of motivation and a loss of interest in the world around her. There were suicidal ideas and feelings of wanting to harm herself . . . loss of self-esteem, which is so undermining, affects your ability to cope with the world.'

He then addressed the added factor of Jane's somewhat undefined child abuse, explaining that the responses of sufferers of a depressive illness, combined with other stresses such as child abuse, are altered. They are more panicky and less able to make clear judgements about what has happened to them. He explained that Jane would have felt powerless, whilst others would have seemed very powerful or much stronger. Her state of mind was equated to being in a grey mist, where she might have been aware of what was happening but powerless. In this misty world 'threats seem much greater and you seem much weaker. Your ability to think clearly is impaired, you may be frozen in panic. You may be unable to decide what to do or to carry through logical plans or decisions.' According to Dr Trevor, it seems that the 'smokescreen' messages were not devious, but were understandable when she was in such a panicky state.

I was amazed at this degree of eloquence and comprehensive analysis from a man who knew Jane for less than four hours. I, who knew her for over four years, would have come to a very different set of conclusions.

Dr Turner summarised by saying that any responsibility for the killing was diminished by the illness from which she was suffering. It is not surprising that the prosecution's expert psychiatrist had a different opinion.

Dr Damian Gamble began rather directly with the opening line of, 'With great respect for Dr Turner's opinion, I do not agree with it . . . I do not think that either the seriousness or the duration of the depressive illness was sufficient to warrant a diagnosis of depressive illness.' Then, when asked by Mr Houlder if Jane's responsibility would have been diminished, he responded resolutely with, 'I do not think so, no.'

And so the court had been offered two diametrically opposed expert opinions which effectively cancelled each other out. The jury sat looking dumbfounded as they stared at these experts.

The prosecution called one last witness, one of five of Tommy's old girlfriends who had offered to testify. All five had expressed regret at the way Jane had portrayed him. None had been molested, and one had experienced consensual anal sex with him.

Mr Houlder was then ready to sum up his case. He told the jury that although it may be a hard job for them, it was 'their duty to find her guilty of murder'. He dismissed her claims of rape and told the jury to 'ask yourselves whether she has made the whole thing up', as she is 'quite clearly a young woman who is capable of telling deliberate lies'. He reminded the jurors that Jane had repeatedly lied to the police and had then continued to lie in the witness box. He summarised the crime as 'a classic case of murder as a result of betrayal', and defined the betrayal as a combination of the e-mails to Debbie and then Thomas's telling her that the relationship was over that Friday in the South of France. He told the jury that Jane was 'a woman who loved, too much, a man who was not yet ready to make the commitment she sought'. It was, said Houlder, 'too much for her to bear'.

The judge then gave his guidance and sent the jury out.

CHAPTER FOURTEEN

THE VERDICT

JANE SAT ASHEN-FACED with large dark bags under her empty eyes. She had rehearsed looking sad and frightened for so long that one wondered if she understood that she had a right to feel that way now. The jury had been out for less than two days, and had reached their verdict. It was now 2.45 p.m. on Wednesday, 16 May. Jane was allowed to sit, without having to ask permission, as she awaited the jurors' decision about the rest of her life. The forewoman stood and announced the majority of the eleven to one verdict.

Jane was guilty of murder.

Her face registered no emotion. She just sat there motionless, dressed in black, clutching at a crumpled tissue. In the courtroom the reactions of the two families were, predictably, quite different. Jane's mother simply mouthed the word 'No . . .' and began to weep. Her father grasped the marble balustrade of the visitors' gallery as tears welled in his eyes. I think everyone in that room pitied them. The Cressmans were justifiably ecstatic. Mr Cressman made a loud sound of pleasure and then gave the victory sign with his hand. He was an old Second World War veteran, but this moment was perhaps his most personal victory, not necessarily because Jane was guilty but because it was now completely clear to the world that his son was innocent.

As Tommy's parents knew, Tom's favourite poem ended with the lines

Life's battle don't always go,

To the stronger or faster man,
But soon or late the man who wins,
Is the man who thinks he can.

Tommy's life was over, but he had won his last battle. His memory had been placed on trial by his murderer – and he had been exonerated. Thomas Cressman could finally rest in peace.

Judge Michael Hyam is a kind, soft-spoken man. He led the trial with compassion and even humour. Now he stared at Jane with hardened eyes and told her, 'Nothing can justify what you did. It was a brutal attack . . . you left him to die without remorse.' He looked straight at Jane's blank face and said, 'In killing the man you loved you ended his life and ruined your own.' Jane was sentenced to life.

A male and female prison officer came towards her and helped her to stand. They escorted her into an awaiting van, where she would be transported back to Holloway prison and placed on suicide watch.

Detective Chief Inspector Jim Dickie was victorious. The last time I saw him he had stared at me with a self-confident look and assured me of the outcome. Jim Dickie was always sure. After the verdict he released a statement expressing his delight with the conviction. He went on to say:

Jane Andrews brutally murdered Tom and then tried to cover her tracks . . . throughout the trial she has tried to destroy Tom's character to portray herself in a more favourable light.

The Metropolitan Police take allegations of domestic violence and rape very seriously, and for Jane Andrews to fabricate such allegations to try to absolve herself of her responsibility for murdering Tom is unforgivable.

The jury came to the right decision.

Barbara Cressman sent me a lovely note expressing her satisfaction with the verdict and enclosed a statement from the Cressman family:

Although the verdict we have just heard will not bring Tom back, we have a conclusion. Our faith in British justice has been rewarded. The jury has confirmed that this was a case of

185

premeditated murder, and that Jane Andrews' lies to cover up her actions were not believed.

Tom was a decent man – a caring and devoted son, brother, uncle, cousin, godfather and friend. All of us who loved him will remember him with pride.

They ended the statement by offering their condolences to Jane's parents: 'At this time we would like to say that we feel sorry for Jane's family, who have effectively lost a daughter.'

Jane might have been truly lost, had she ever truly existed. But she was too afraid of reality to really live. She created her own world and lived in her lies. It was no wonder that she could vilify her victim. Murdering Thomas had not satisfied her anger at a man unwilling to accompany her into her fantasy world. For that, she needed to attack his ghost. She had fortunately failed to convince a jury of her peers, but I am sure that she convinced herself. With whom does she share her cell in Holloway prison? Does Heathcliff visit her there on Penistone Crag? Maybe it does not matter; for Jane has escaped Grimsby at last.

INDEX

Note: No entry is given for Jane Dunn-Butler (Andrews) as she appears consistently throughout the book.